DEDICATI

To a better understanding and a fuller life for all the Lees and
Dannys in the world.

Down But Not Out

A TRUE STORY BY

Elizabeth Berns

First published in
New Zealand in 2004 by
National Pacific Press
PO Box 57-202
Mana 6230
Porirua, New Zealand
Ph 64 4 233 8204
E-mail: books@npp.co.nz

ISBN 1-877368-01-6

Text and cover artwork by Hutcheson, Bowman and Stewart, Wellington.

Cover design concept by National Pacific Press.

Printed by Hutcheson, Bowman and Stewart.

ACKNOWLEDGEMENTS

My thanks to everyone who so thoughtfully and unselfishly gave of their time for the many interviews for this book.

About the Author

Elizabeth Berns has had a varied career, which has included working in graphic and commercial arts, copywriting, journalism and public relations. Her diverse interests embrace writing poetry and prose, drawing and painting as well as a strong armchair interest in sport, particularly Formula One motor racing.

Elizabeth has three married children and several grandchildren, one of whom is the subject of this book.

Elizabeth currently resides in Auckland, New Zealand.

PREFACE

Talking with and about Lee, in this account of her life, is an attempt to understand the joys and the trials of a young girl with Down syndrome as she moves through her childhood and becomes a young adult. What this young woman thinks and feels about growing up. How her thoughts, needs and emotions conform with, or differ from, normal girls of her own age. Lee and I discussed this at some length during a number of conversations we have had together, and hopefully we have found some answers. Her responses have ranged from being extremely funny to being very sad. The changes in her emotions have often been quite swift and this has frequently made it difficult for us and for her to cope with. Life can become a difficult and volatile mixture when the limitations imposed from having Down syndrome are combined with the usual fluctuations of teenage hormones. Her progress has needed empathetic support and involvement from the whole family whenever and wherever possible. However, this period is not all gloom and doom, it has a wonderful light side which we have all enjoyed.

Lee has grown into a young girl with a surprisingly rich understanding of herself, her needs and of her surroundings. She has a gentle sense of humour, a sense of fun and is sensitive to criticism and praise alike. Now, at eighteen years old, she has become an interesting and interested participant in the society in which she lives. As Lee developed it became clear to us that she has understood much more than she has been capable of expressing. It is still almost impossible to gauge the floor or the ceiling of her intake because her expression of it is hampered by a lack of suitable vocabulary, and frequently by her inability to grasp the connection between complex actions and their consequences. However, these drawbacks have not impaired her sense of fun or her sense of humour.

She has made me rethink the idea that people who have Down syndrome are unaware of their condition and its limitations, for it seems they are not. This is one of the heart-wrenching aspects of this condition. There may be some truth in the saying that you cannot miss what you have never had, but it does not prevent you from wanting what you have not got, however unattainable it may be.

Apart from the conversations we have had together, to tell as complete a story as possible, it has been necessary to introduce a number of interviews with the various people that Lee comes into constant contact with. These include her family, friends, teachers, siblings and her boyfriend.

We have started with Lee's birth and how it affected the family and how these early years may have influenced her subsequent development. However, watching this fledgling adult make as smooth and as untroubled a transition as possible into the woman she hopes to be, is the focus of the story.

Lee was most enthusiastic when we first discussed writing her story and whilst she has remained an interested and willing participant in it, she very soon indicated that she definitely preferred her contribution to come from the discussions and 'interviews' we shared. Sitting at the computer and writing parts of it herself was not what she had in mind. We have had a lot of fun and laughter during our talks but because her interest is spasmodic and is not able to be sustained for long periods, the principal format is peppered with anecdotal inserts.

In sections of dialogue with Lee throughout the story, Down syndrome is frequently referred to as Down's, a term Lee prefers to use. In this regard it should be noted that in the late 1970s it was decided by the American medical community that the apostrophe-s should be removed from diseases, and that conditions be named after the discoverer rather than of the person with the condition. Notwithstanding this decision, the apostrophe-s remains in European usage.

Finally, while this is a true story, the names of most people within it have been changed in order to preserve their privacy.

Reference:

Why Down and not Down's? Margaret A. Fitzgerald, MS, RN, CS, FAANP

http://www.pcc.com/lists/pedalk.archive/0205/00020.html

PART ONE

THE EARLY YEARS

I wanted to write a book about myself, about being born Down's, but it is difficult to say what I think, so I have asked my grandma to help me. It's not easy being Down's.

I was born in August 1983. Two of my brothers had already been born, so my mum was delighted to find that she now had a daughter. What she had not expected was that I would be Down's. Because she was only twenty-nine when I was born, she had not been tested for this possibility.

My gran, who was at the hospital on the day I arrived, says that I was born with a similar amount of fuss and pushing and hurting as my brothers had been. The doctor made some excuse to her as he whisked me away before we had a proper chance to meet each other, but Mum, who is really called Janet, was not too bothered about this at the time. She had just given birth to me, and was pleased that it was all over. She needed to rest. I have seen from films what a hard job it is to have a baby, so I know how tired it must have made her.

Gran says that later that morning the doctor put his head around the door and gave my mother a smile. Then, looking directly at my dad, he said, 'Can I have a word?' just like the police do on TV in "The Bill".

When they were outside the ward he told my dad that I had Down syndrome, and that they would not give me any 'heroic treatment' if it became necessary. My gran had better explain it all.

On a cold August morning in 1983, when the sun, bright but without warmth, spread its lemon light over the dry dawn landscape, Lee was born. The leafless trees stood still in the light breezes that fingered them. This was to be a day on which more than one life was to take on a new shape.

Janet, flushed and radiant after Lee's birth, waited for her new daughter to be brought to her. She had seen baby Lee being taken into an adjacent room where she expected that they would be cleaning her up. What she had not realised was that Lee was being carefully examined by her gynaecologist, who had immediately called in a paediatrician to examine her further. Tenderly the paediatrician had run his hands over Lee's tiny body, pausing, testing her little limbs, turning her head from one side to the other. Then after feeling the nape of her neck with the tips of his fingers, he gently laid her back on the bed. His hands had moved over the little figure with a sculptor's certainty, and he understood what the contours were indicating. Smiling down at the tiny baby, he combed his fingers slowly through her hair. Then he looked up and, with a slight nod, he confirmed the gynaecologist's opinion — baby Lee had Down syndrome. Through the glass doors the two doctors could be seen chatting and nodding to each other. Finally, the paediatrician left and it was the unhappy task of Janet's gynaecologist to break the news and to explain the prognosis to the new parents. And just as Lee said, David, my son-in-law, was asked out 'to have a word'. A sad emotional discussion followed.

'Have you spoken to my wife?' my stunned son-in-law asked.

'Not yet. I thought I would discuss it with you first.'

The joy he had felt when he heard that they now had a daughter slowly turned to disbelief, as the doctor explained that due to a genetic aberration, their baby had been born with Down syndrome.

'I am deeply sorry, Mr Jackson, but there is nothing we can do to alter this condition.'

He carried on explaining and comforting, but David was past hearing. It was all happening too quickly for him, and he was devastated. Tears ran down his face. How was he going to tell Janet, who had just spent the last few hours in agony producing this baby, and nine months before that planning and waiting for her? The doctor was patient and sympathetic.

'Come, Mr Jackson. We'll talk to your wife together.'

David felt removed from the reality around him. He had the feeling that he was walking in a cocoon as he followed the doctor into the ward where Janet was finishing a cup of tea. Although she looked tired, she still glowed with the radiance of motherhood. David looked away.

'Mrs Jackson, I'm afraid the news is not very good,' the doctor started to say.

Janet, sensing danger, interrupted. 'What's going on? Where's my baby? Is she all right?'

'I'm afraid not, Mrs Jackson. I mean she seems to be all right, but I called in a paediatrician to examine her to make sure, you see.' He paused, then looking down into Janet's worried eyes, he continued almost in a whisper as if afraid to say the words.

'I believe she has Down syndrome.'

'What does that mean?' Janet asked, puzzled.

She looked at David who turned towards the window, unable to return her look. She redirected her question to the doctor.

'What does that mean?'

Before he could answer a young nurse entered, carrying a tiny swaddled bundle which she placed in Janet's arms. She looked at the little face, still red from its fight into life, and fell in love. She turned to the doctor who had already started going through the explanation he had previously given to David. Placing his hand gently on Janet's shoulder, David stood beside her bed, still unable to speak as he fought to keep back his tears. When the doctor had finished reciting the causes and possible problems the baby's future may hold, he reiterated the offer of non-heroic treatment that he had made to David. At this point Janet flared up.

'Oh no, you do everything you can for my baby, just as you would for any other baby.'

The doctor, surprised by her conviction, agreed to do his best. So baby Lee had her first reprieve.

Left alone, the new parents recovered together. They were both aware that something momentous, though unclear and unspoken, had happened in their lives. They felt isolated, detached and rudderless. And Janet still felt angry with her doctor.

'I can't believe he said that,' she said, holding out her hand towards her husband.

David moved closer to her. He looked round for a chair, his legs feeling weak. Reluctant to move away from Janet's side, he sat down on the bed and taking her outstretched hand, buried his face in it. He was inconsolable. His wife did not deserve this.

'David, what's wrong with you? Things can't always be perfect.' Janet hesitated. She had never seen her husband so visibly shattered. 'What if she had been born perfect, then had an accident and was no longer the perfect child we'd had? Would we then abandon her to a no-treatment vacuum?'

'Of course not, Janet.'

'Well?'

Janet did not reveal what she was feeling during those moments of discovery, perhaps not even to herself. She had set the rules and she was going to abide by them.

A few days later, baby Lee, unaware of the drama that had heralded her arrival, slept soundly in Janet's arms as David drove them home. Their lives had now moved off the axis they had been used to living on. Both knew that their future was about to change, but neither knew how.

◆◆⋉◆◆

Home was a sunny house that overlooked a large, leafy garden. Lee's two older brothers, Jake and Jason, each had a room of their own. However, Janet felt that until she was more secure about how little Lee was going to progress it would be better to have her close by. Her crib therefore replaced the bedside table in Janet and David's room. But as it happened, Lee was a model newborn baby. She slept and ate well, and spent many happy hours suckling on Janet's ever-present milk supply. As Janet became more confident, she moved the boys into a large shared room and Lee was given her own room. There was no complaint from the boys, who carried on playing, fighting and laughing.

It is possible that when you are closely involved in a situation, it does not occur to you to question the events that you have witnessed, believing that what you saw was exactly what had happened. So it has taken eighteen years for questions to be asked of David, questions relating to his feelings and reactions during those early days after Lee's birth. During a recent conversation concerning this story, David has made this enormous part of his life accessible to me.

◆◆⋉◆◆

After Lee's birth so many questions, with answers that were difficult to find, were asked. Why has this happened to Lee? How will Lee's condition affect the boys? Will Janet manage? How are we going to manage? The circles of questions became woven into circles of answers and predictions. Slowly, each member of the family found their own answer. And no one, except perhaps Janet, had seen or understood the depth of David's misery.

Being a positive, confident person, David has always felt that he could tackle any problem that might confront him and he has subsequently proven this to be so. However, on this occasion he was overcome by the helplessness of his position. There was nothing he could do to put things right. An inconsolable feeling of isolation reinforced the devastation that he felt. As there was absolutely nothing he could do to change the situation, he had to find a way of accepting it. But because he did not know anyone who had any experience of parenting a handicapped child, he felt acutely alone and became trapped in his own bewilderment.

'David, when Lee was born, what sort of things were going through your mind?'

'Well, for example, how was our life about to change, what sort of lifestyle could we all expect to lead, with a focus that always needed to consider this child first? And more than that, how would we handle it if we became a socially unacceptable family? I had no idea what to expect in terms of behaviour from a child with Down syndrome.'

As we spoke, the intensity of the whole experience returned and flooded through him. Although he was still looking at me, his eyes seemed to refocus inwards as he unlocked the memory of those events and the feelings they had roused in him. As the memories gushed back his face became strained.

'It was all a frightening mystery.'

'What about Janet?'

'Janet may have been crying inside, but she projected a pragmatic presence which had a stabilising effect. She also went about organising help, and gathering around us people who were in the same boat as we were.'

'Where did you find that the most help came from?'

'Unquestionably from people who had a child with Down's, especially one older than ours. I had a great sense of failure because I knew I could do absolutely nothing to fix this.'

David paused, and a wistful look of sadness touched his face as he continued. 'You see I have usually managed to fix most things, but I knew that this was going to be different. I would have to redefine my goals and expectations for this particular child.'

'Do you think on a personal level that you have succeeded in doing this?'

'Perhaps, maybe it's been a growing experience.'

'I have heard that the birth and the rearing of a handicapped child can break up a seemingly happy and united family? Do you think that at any time you were in danger of this happening to you?'

'On the contrary, I think it has made us all much stronger. Even the boys have become more aware, protective and understanding of people with disabilities and I'm sure it will help them in later life. It's had a positive influence on the family. It's made us look at ourselves and dig deeper.'

'You're right. It's done that for me too.'

At this point I thought that our discussion was over, and I certainly did not expect the passionate honesty that followed.

'Before we finish, there is something I want to say.' Without waiting for a reply David continued, 'I just want to tell you that right at the beginning I could not get over the grief. I would find myself howling in the shower. I was overwhelmed with grief. This was the biggest thing I'd had to deal with, ever. I felt so helpless, I had no idea how to attack this or deal with it, where to turn. This was the biggest challenge in my life. The intensity of that pain and that grief stayed with me, and it only started to ease after about six months.'

We shared a quiet moment of grief before returning to the present.

'What about now that Lee is an eighteen-year-old young adult? How do you feel?'

'Great, she's doing well. But there are times when I feel a huge sympathy for her being a teenager.'

'It's always been difficult to be a teenager.'

'Yes, but for her it is even more difficult because she can't express her worries or even hope to understand them. Unlike most teenagers, she doesn't have a confidante or a bunch of peers to share her girls' stuff with, so she just keeps it to herself and suffers it.'

The unexpected intimacy of all that had been said and shared left us each separately and silently embracing its meaning.

A riot of colour warmed the walls in Lee's bedroom. Paper Christmas decorations arched over her crib. The winter sun shafted through the big bay window's leadlight panes, and fell in a shower of sunny squares against the opposite wall. Nearby, a pile of cuddly toys waited to befriend their new owner. Janet had begun what was to become a lifelong effort to generate and surround Lee with a range of stimuli.

Meanwhile, Lee was fast becoming a model baby. She fed, slept and smiled blissfully up into her mother's face. They were getting to know each other, while the rest of the family was still trying to understand what was happening. After the initial shock began to fade, we started to wonder what we were in for and how we were going to handle it. We were in unknown territory, with no previous experience of dealing with mentally or physically impaired children, or with the parents of such children. We desperately needed to find a direction.

Our concerns were shared by a number of our friends. Being unsure of how to approach Janet and David, many of them telephoned to ask my advice. Should they congratulate them, and should they still give Janet the gifts that they had purchased for the baby? When I consulted her about this, Janet's positive and loving attitude set the tone that she has maintained ever since.

'Of course they should.' She paused a moment, then added. 'Why should they be in doubt?'

She wanted them to come, to visit us and to meet our new baby, and perhaps more than anything to just be their normal selves.

Janet's friends began calling. At first they seemed nervous and careful about how they phrased their comments about baby Lee. Because of Janet's positive attitude their restraint soon passed and they became more relaxed and uninhibited. She explained as best she could about Down syndrome and how it came about, and then went on to discuss the usual new baby 'stuff' mothers talk about. Her attitude was rewarded with warmth and support as they quite openly admired her strength.

When they saw baby Lee, they melted with love just as we had done. She was changing. Like a butterfly, she was slowly emerging from her ruddy newborn chrysalis state into a beautiful baby. A shock of dark brown hair stood straight up all over her head, forming a silky frame around her chubby little face and highlighting two of the pinkest cheeks a baby could have. Our baby was taking on a persona.

'Do you want to write something now, Lee?'

'Not really, you can do it. Gran, I think my brothers weren't really interested in babies, but when they saw that I was different they became interested in me. Isn't that right, Gran?'

'I don't think so darling. I think they were just pleased to have a sister.'

These questions fall from a deep mysterious cloud of pain that occasionally passes over Lee, giving us a fleeting insight into her thoughts. She seems unable to verbally enlarge on these thoughts, but may possibly do so in her mind.

Lee's perception held a measure of truth, but because her brothers knew very little about babies, their interest in her being different was momentary.

'Mum, what will being Down's do to Lee? What does it mean?' Jake asked about his sister.

'We don't really know what effect it will have on her yet, but we hope it won't be too drastic.'

'Like what?' Jake was persistent.

'It could be anything from a weak chest to a big heart problem. Don't worry about it now, we'll just have to wait and hope for the best.'

Satisfied with Janet's reply, Jake went off to his room to tackle his Lego set. His younger brother, Jason, who was only two years older than Lee, thought she was 'okay' and left it at that. However, Jake continued to display a mild interest in her. His interest, which waned as time passed, was clearly expressed in his final pronouncement on her.

'Babies don't do much, do they mum?'

'Gran?'

'Yes, Lee?'

'You know that my mother's always right.'

'That's news to me.'

'Oh please, Gran, of course she is.'

Lee was in the mood to continue.

'My mother even knows what's right for you, Gran. When I need to know anything I can ask her and she has the answer. Like the other day when you asked me if I would like to go out for tea, and I had to explain it to you all over again.'

'But I was asking you, Lee.'

'I know, and I said you must ask Janet, because she'll know.'

'But I want to know what you think.'

'Don't be silly, Gran. My mother knows, just ask her.'

I don't know why my gran can't understand that my mother is the one to ask. I can't make these sorts of decisions. I don't mind if we stay home or if we go out. It's not because I don't like going out, but it's because I have stuff that I enjoy doing at home. Anyway, it makes me really cross when she goes on about it. People don't usually ask me what I want to do, they tell me what the thing to do is and I do it. I don't like making decisions.

Lee is right, it has always been difficult to elicit a definite decision from her. If she is interested in a suggestion she usually says 'maybe', and waits to be told the next step, which she usually takes. This could be because as she was growing up she was not really given many options on which to decide. On the other hand, when she was given a choice she frequently ignored the offer. Ignoring suggestions or comments is one of the mechanisms Lee employs to escape from situations she feels she cannot handle.

However, most of the time, choice has not been a major problem. The only area in which Lee makes a quick positive decision is in her choice of clothing. She knows exactly what she wants to wear and is not easily dissuaded. Lee, like most teenagers, would be the best one to explain her dress sense.

I'm not a child and the adults in my house don't understand what girls want to wear. I know what colours I like, and I also know what other colours look good with them. I think black is a great colour and all the girls at my school wear it. I also like blue and red and I know how to match them. My mother says that I know how to put together a good-looking outfit, even though I sometimes get the weather wrong and end up too hot. It's funny, but I don't often feel cold. Mum feels it for me.

When I was small I kept on changing my clothes, but I don't think that my mum was really angry with me for this, because I heard her telling my gran one day that I was just like my brothers who also went through this stage. What's more, she didn't even fuss when I took them all off because I was hot. I remember once, when I had thrown them all off, she let me play on the lawn under the sprinkler. I loved that and we all laughed a lot. Even the dog joined in and got wet.

'Can I tell them about him, Gran?'

'Of course you can, Lee, but remember that she was a girl and not a boy dog.'

'I know that.'

'Right. Carry on.'

'He was a great big black Great Dane called Sheba and he didn't mind when I sat on him or cuddled him, although he was taller than me. Sometimes when we walked around the garden together he let me put my arm around his neck and we walked together like friends do. I'm not sure what happened to him because my mother said that he died. I don't know why, but I'm afraid of dogs now, even the small ones. I quite like cats, so my mother bought me one for my birthday. His name is Lucy and he's old and he doesn't like anyone to touch him. He sometimes lets me pat his head, but I'm afraid of him because he has a quick temper.'

'Lee, why did you call Sheba and Lucy "he" when you know that they are both "she"?'

'That's what I said.'

'Well, it's not what I heard.'

'That's your problem, Gran.'

Although Lee is well aware of gender differences, for some reason she generally prefers to use masculine pronouns. On rare occasions she does say 'she', so it is not that she cannot pronounce the 'sh' sound, although she may not feel comfortable using her tongue in that position. If this is so, it does not explain why she also shies away from using 'her'. Two other explanations are possible. One is that she has not grasped the concept, and the other is that she does not really care to be that exact. My questioning interrupted her flow and put her out considerably.

'I am still talking for the book, Gran!' she said, informing and asking me at the same time.

'Yes, go on.'

'I'm finished.'

'But you said you were still talking?'

'I know, but now I'm not, I'm finished.'

With that, Lee got up and headed for the security of her bedroom. She definitely does not accept criticism easily.

Because babies with Down syndrome are usually "floppy" due to poor muscle tone, Janet was advised to pay special attention to exercising Lee. She tried to accomplish this with a regular routine of extending and flexing her little arms and legs as she lay on her towel after her bath. She seemed to be double-jointed, but this was really a sign of her poor muscle tone. Lee quite passively accepted the movements and gurgled her way through the sessions. But because progress was slow, Janet decided to try a few swimming lessons as a booster exercise.

She found a teacher who specialised in teaching babies to swim, which in real terms meant teaching them to turn over onto their backs and float. Doggy paddle came much later. Denise, the teacher, had a small warmed indoor pool filled with a nervous clutch of mothers who laughed and cajoled their babies into action as she called out a series of instructions. It was a noisy affair as the babies cried, coughed and spluttered their way through the lessons. Their ages ranged from a few weeks to twelve months old. Lee fitted into the 'few weeks' category, being five weeks old at the time. She had no fear of water, so it was not long before she qualified to be 'dropped' into the pool from just above the water. Her surprise at this sudden turn of events quickly gave way to the 'training' as she turned over onto her back. Janet stood by in the water, arms outstretched to rescue her if need be.

The most stressed group were definitely the mothers, who needed constant reassuring that their babies would not drown themselves. Lee, like the other small babies, had to wear a disposable nappy under her tiny blue swimsuit as the exercise did what it was intended to do, stimulating the muscles, including the bowels. It was not long before our little bundle was a water baby.

Lee has subsequently become the best swimmer in the family. These days she swims competitively and has won a number of ribbons for her team. Although she is a member of a team, Lee is definitely not a team player.

'Can I say something here, Gran?'

'Sure, go ahead.'

'I still enjoy swimming, but getting undressed and dressed again and then having to have my hair washed afterwards is a big nuisance. You can go on now, Gran.'

Meanwhile, to her brothers at home, Lee had become just another baby in the house. Looked at, played with and tolerated. Everyone was getting on with their own lives.

Over the years Lee's eyesight and hearing have appeared to be reasonably normal. At one time we had thought that her hearing may have been defective, but this turned out to be selective. She 'failed to hear' the things she was not interested in responding to. Indeed, her health has only once given us great cause for concern. When Lee was three years old she was admitted to hospital with a serious bout of pneumonia. She was extremely ill and needed to be placed in an oxygen tent to assist her breathing. Janet, still remembering her doctor's earlier warning, refused to leave her bedside even for a few minutes. She wanted to be absolutely sure that the so-called 'heroic treatment' would definitely be provided.

This episode, which had threatened Lee's life, deeply affected Janet. She seemed to have come through it with a closer and an even more heightened sense of responsibility for Lee. For a time she nervously made quite sure that she got immediate medical attention if she so much as sneezed. Her concern has not waned over the years, as Lee's health is still one of Janet's major priorities. In some mysterious way it seems as if Janet and Lee share the same life force.

<hr />

My gran says that I was a good baby. I suppose that meant that I ate my food and didn't cry a lot, although she says I was a bit slow in learning to sit up, crawl and even to walk. Talking was a real problem for me. My tongue kept getting in the way, so it was difficult to say the words I wanted to say. When I wasn't talking or doing anything, maybe just sitting around, my mum kept on telling me to close my mouth. She couldn't have known how uncomfortable that was for me, because my mouth felt so full up from my tongue. Well, perhaps she did realise it eventually, because I was taken to see a doctor who operated on my tongue and made it smaller. It was sore but it got better very quickly, and I'm pleased we did it because now I speak quite well and I've even got my own cell phone.

'Gran?'

'Yes.'

'What does my mother say when I phone her at the shops?'

'Hello.'

'Oh, please.' We both have a giggle.

'You mean when we're at the supermarket and you want her to buy more stuff?'

'So?'

'Well she buys it, doesn't she?'

'I know that.'

'Well if you know that, why worry about it? Why don't you write it all down on her shopping list?'

'I do, but sometimes I forget.'

'I already know your favourites.'

'Like what?'

'Like apple rings, popcorn and tomato sauce.'

'So, don't you understand, I need them.'

Lee makes good use of her cell phone. If she gets out of school early she rings Janet, and if she cannot get her she calls me. Janet does not care how often or for what trivia she uses her phone, she's just delighted that Lee thinks about using it and can do so when she wants or needs to.

───◆◆►◄◆◆───

When the decision was made to operate on Lee's tongue, the doctor had also offered Janet a cosmetic procedure which could change the shape of her eyes and give them a more conventional appearance. After much discussion it was decided, rightly or wrongly, not to have that operation for two reasons. Firstly, it could be risking her health for the sake of a purely cosmetic procedure. A secondary consideration was that making her appearance more conventional could make her life more difficult in the long run, as more would be expected from her than she was capable of doing. This could put her into potentially stressful or even dangerous situations. Lee was, at that time, too young to be consulted.

───◆◆►◄◆◆───

When Lee was a toddler, Janet enrolled her at a play school. It was not a 'special school' and Lee was the only child there with Down syndrome. By now the boys had lost interest in the new baby and Lee needed playmates. The problem was that she was taking a long time to become potty-trained. The school staff were extremely understanding, and as long as Janet included an emergency pack of underwear in Lee's little case, they coped.

Having Lee at school for a few hours every day gave Janet some time to herself. Lee was happy there. She spent most of her day digging in the sandpit, playing with toys, and having milk and biscuits. Before going home they all had to lie down to rest on little mats, during which time Lee invariably fell asleep. Her days were much like those of the other children, except that she did not speak to any of them and simply ignored them when they spoke to her. Was she shy or self-protecting? Perhaps she did not understand them, or maybe it was a combination of all of these things and others we were not aware of. We were never sure.

In the long run, communication with the other children did not become a huge problem for her or for them, as they were mostly engaged in watching each other and in individual play. The real contact between them all came from bouts of crying, pulling and pushing when toys were snatched or coveted. Through this fighting Lee was being introduced to some sort of 'socialising' which she had not encountered until then. At this, her first school, Lee may have learnt that she would not always be the centre of attention as she was at home.

'Shall I tell them about your next school?'

'Maybe.'

'Is that a "yes" or a "no", Lee?'

'Well, if you like.'

'Would you like to tell them yourself?'

'No, I can't remember it. Gran, you didn't tell them about Molly.'

'What about Molly?'

'You know.'

'You know more about it than I do, so you explain it.'

'Well let me see, oh I know, we were playing and Molly ran in front of me and I fell over her and broke my front tooth. That's all.'

'Not quite, Lee. You forgot to say that Molly was a small what?'

'Dog of course, Gran. You can be so silly. I knew that all the time!'

Lee had to stay at home for a while between schools, as the nursery school could not take her until she was fully potty-trained. This was not an easy matter to overcome, for although she seemed to understand the concept she did not have the bladder control to go with it. It was more a question of time than training. Janet hoped that this would turn out to be a minor hurdle. Still, not knowing how long it would take before Lee could start at her new school, Janet decided to contact the local (then South African) Down Society to find out what was generally available.

Through them she made contact with other mothers who lived nearby and whose babies had Down syndrome. She decided to invite them over, hoping that their gathering would develop into a social group for like-minded people, and that together they could form a club and hopefully do something interesting for their children.

The 'club' produced some surprising members. Until we eventually met each other, we had thought that Down syndrome children were born to older parents, yet the people that responded and later became a close harmonious group of friends were all under thirty years old, the youngest being a mother of only nineteen. The formation of this group proved to be of great benefit to all of us — children, parents and grandparents alike. We started by meeting for evening coffee at a different house each month. I remember that first night. We started with five couples and two grandmothers. At first we were all rather shy of each other, and only managed the usual meaningless small talk that gets people through this sort of event. But during the coffee break, as we stood around the dining room table, the conversations became more intimate.

'So how long have you been married?'

'How many children have you got?'

And finally the crucial question was asked.

'Which of your children is the Down's baby?'

It was a moment of self-recognition, of confirmation, and for each parent it was rather like coming out of the closet or standing up and publicly admitting that one was an alcoholic. It was a public declaration of being the parent of a child with Down syndrome. It meant moving out of the comfort and understanding of one's own family circle. It was about being comfortable, and being able to speak openly and freely without waiting for the awkward moments that inevitably followed the mention of Down syndrome. The question opened the sluice gates, and a flood of information flowed between this group of special parents, infusing them with strength and self-confidence. After that night we knew that we had begun to travel in a direction that would bear fruit for us all.

As our meetings progressed, we discussed the headway that our children were or were not making. Useful subjects were opened and probed, and painful questions were being uncovered and discussed. Questions like: 'How do you feel when you go out with your child in public?' and 'What sort of effect is your child having on its siblings?'

Most of us did not have any trouble with sibling relationships, which ranged from normal jealousy of the new arrival, to acceptance, or even disinterest. The exception was one couple, who were unable to accept what they regarded as 'a difficult predicament'. Going out with Lee was not an issue for us. The biggest problem we all faced was a far more practical one, toilet training. This became our most frequently examined topic, as no one had any idea how to explain the concept. One mum said that she had tried by showing her daughter how to sit on the potty, but that she had laughed so much that it became a favourite seat for her toddler who carried it around with her toys. It was a start. However, a much more far-reaching problem, which we were all hoping to overcome, was the lack of company for the children. Initially we were able to conquer this by arranging weekend gatherings at one of our houses. But beyond that, it was to remain a rather sad problem for a very long time.

These weekend BBQs gave the fathers a chance to relax together. They seemed to have a much more difficult time accepting the fact that they had children with Down syndrome than their wives had. They gave each other a great deal of strength and understanding during those smoky hours spent around the BBQ burning the sausages. That they were able to share a social event and to talk about their children, and even laugh at some of their antics, was a huge relief for them. The fact that each accepted the other without question or embarrassment played a very important part in rebuilding their confidence.

The children's health was also a major concern to the group. Some of them were developing hearing problems, others needed glasses, and respiratory infections frequently invaded their tiny chests. One little mite had a serious heart problem and would probably need to have surgery to correct it. All this was openly discussed and the concern was shared and borne by all. The undercurrent of unspoken understanding provided the stabilising base we had all been seeking.

When the children became used to each other they began to enjoy being together. During these weekend gatherings they played, fought and cried. A semblance of normality had crept into those days; they had become just a bunch of friends chatting, laughing and relaxing together. However, after the group had become well-established, and the various social adjustments had been made, it was time to take another step. But where to next? The future seemed to be an open blur. What could we do for them? How were we going to teach the children, and *what* were we going to teach them?

'Dr Spock for Children with Down Syndrome' had not been written. Janet decided to investigate further. Information from the internet had not become available yet, so she started writing to universities around the world, requesting information. Her first reply came from the head of a university department who offered advice and a reading list. Among the names on the list was that of a Birmingham father, Rex Brinkworth MBE, who, as a psychologist, had studied and documented a heap of information about his own daughter, who had Down syndrome. In the 1970s he had founded the United Kingdom's first Down Syndrome Association. Apart from his studies on the possible benefits of various supplements to aid the development of children with Down syndrome, he worked tirelessly to overcome prevalent establishment attitudes and allow these children to reach their full potential. His daughter had progressed to become a typist. This news brought the group tremendous encouragement, and together they raised the money to bring him out from England. He not only gave them the lead they were seeking, but also gave a very enlightening public lecture.

All this activity refreshed and invigorated the group. It had been given a direction, which could be followed or varied accordingly. It had suddenly become thinkable that our children may have the potential to develop much further than any of us had previously thought possible. It had even become feasible that they may one day be able to integrate reasonably well into society. It was clearly understood that this would require a big commitment. The children would need to be constantly stimulated, directed and taught, and this would also apply to the acquisition of social skills.

There was much to do, and all but one couple was willing to put in the effort. The abstaining couple eventually decided to place their child in a home for special needs care. They had been unable to come to terms with the part that they needed to play in the personal care of their child. Neither path is an easy one.

As the children grew older the group disintegrated, but it had served its purpose and the families moved on. Some left to live overseas, others got divorced. Having a child with a disability has a major impact on the nuclear family and, to a lesser extent, the entire family circle. The importance of having support from a group of people in similar circumstances had proved its worth. It had given these young families the strength to get on with their lives.

Lee walked into the sitting room with a big photo album under her arm. Sitting down beside me, she rapidly paged through the glossy sleeves until she found pictures of the two of us. For a moment she just studied the pictures and then she looked up into my face.

'I love looking at these old pictures, Gran. I can see you, and you look different.'

'How do I look different, Lee?'

She considered the photographs, and ran her fingers over the pictures of herself.

'That's me.'

'I can see that, Lee, but you haven't answered my question.'

She looked at me, put her head on one side, and then gave a big smile.

'You've got much more wrinkles.'

'Thank you very much, Lee. I needed that to make my day.'

We both laughed.

'Well it's true, Gran,' she confirmed.

Eventually school beckoned, but there was some uncertainty as to where to send Lee. Should she go to a school where there were other disabled children and where she would not have the pressure of facing faster-minded peers? Endless discussions followed. Her bladder control had improved to the extent that she could hold out until she reached the official toilet break time. A spare set of underwear tucked away in her little school bag was provided for any occasional lapses.

Because small children with Down syndrome appear to learn a great deal from copying rather than from assimilating what they are being taught, a special school was ruled out. Lee joined a small group of children of her own age at the Montessori school, which was situated in the friendly environment of a rambling old mansion. This proved to be the right choice for her, and in fact was a huge success. She learnt valuable life skills there, without which she would have been further handicapped.

The children spent a great deal of time dressing and undressing, using their own clothes or trying out the fancy-dress clothes from the school's collection. These simple and extremely popular activities taught them to cope with buttons, fasteners, zippers and bows. They washed small items of clothing in tubs of warm soapy water, and then they rinsed and pegged them to a low, reachable clothesline to dry. To our surprise they were allowed to use a fairly hot iron to press them. Lee loved the ironing, she was gentle and careful, and managed not to burn herself. Most of her day was spent either ironing or baking biscuits. However, at this time she developed a puzzling problem. For no obvious reason she began to hit some of the children.

During the first five years of her schooling, Lee went through various behavioural cycles. From being shy, she quite unexpectedly became defensive. The reason for this was never clearly established. Janet suspected that she might have been bullied or even shunned. The possibility also existed that she may have done something to annoy one of the children, who hit her. This would have greatly surprised her as she had never been smacked or hit, so the whole experience could have unnerved her.

Some of this anti-social behaviour may also have been due to the huge frustration Lee was experiencing at not being able to adequately express herself verbally. Whatever the cause was, the result of her new belligerence was disturbing and could not be allowed to develop, especially as Lee, like many children with Down syndrome, was physically strong.

The school was put on alert, and the teachers went to great lengths to prevent Lee from being provoked in any way. This was also to protect the other children, of course. Janet spoke to Lee about hitting out at people, explaining that she was not going to make friends if she continued being nasty. She seemed oblivious to this reasoning.

However, exactly why this change in Lee's behaviour occurred remains a mystery, as she simply slipped out of that phase as if it had never happened. She has never hit out at anyone since. Instead, she becomes deeply pained, introspective and tearful if she is verbally or emotionally hurt.

Mostly she has enjoyed being at school, and has been willing, though perhaps not eager, to go each day.

Lee walked into the room and sat down on the settee next to me. I held out my arms and she snuggled into them.

'Are you bored, Lee?'

'Not really.' She stroked my arm.

'Do you feel like a chat for our book?'

'If you like.'

'I like.'

'Oh Gran, what are you talking about?'

'You asked me if I felt like talking, so I said "yes".'

'That didn't sound like you said "yes".'

'I know. I was just playing with you.'

'I knew that. What do you want to talk about?'

'How about school?'

'I don't think so.'

'Ok then, what about your school when you were in South Africa?'

'If you like. My teacher was very old, like you.'

'Thanks very much!'

Lee, laughing, snuggled in closer and then sat up and looked serious.

'Okay, I'm ready.'

Lee's concentration seemed focused, and the opportunity was too ripe to waste on a general conversation.

'Let's go back to your first school when you were a tiny little girl.'

Lee giggled, so perhaps the idea of being a tiny little girl amused her.

'Lee, do you think people should smack or hit other people?'

'I don't know.' She shrugged, surprised by the question.

'You must have some idea.'

'Well, I suppose not.'

'Would you hit someone?'

She shook her head.

'Gran, you mustn't ask me that.'

'Well, would you?'

'I already told you. Of course not.'

'When you were small you sometimes smacked some of the children in your class at school. Do you remember that?'

Lee looked over to Janet.

'Tell your mother to stop saying that.'

'You tell her yourself.'

'But she's your mother.'

After that definitive statement Lee regarded the conversation as closed.

The next school was the real thing. It was the neighbourhood primary school and Lee was the only child there who had Down syndrome. There were no special facilities or teacher aids. The prevailing attitudes, and the lack of understanding at that time, simply did not provide for any helpful accommodation of children with Down syndrome in the government school system.

If Lee was not going to attend a special school for handicapped children, then she would have to fit in as best she could. This was not all bad, as she was surrounded by a bunch of normal healthy children from whom she picked up some good and some bad habits. The children were kind to her, even though she did her best to ignore them. The pace of their day was not one she could keep up with, so she opted out. So much for cultivating friends.

Although the school was within walking distance of her house, Janet preferred to drive down to the school. She always parked close to the gate in the shade of a huge old oak tree, which protected her from the strong mid-day sun. Lee knew where to look for the car. Janet made sure that she was always there before the home-time bell rang.

One day she arrived at the school to find that, for some unknown reason, the children had all been let out early and Lee was not at the gate. Janet left the car where it was, hoping that Lee would see it and wait there for her. She rushed into the school to look for her. The school was almost empty, except for a group of young girls sitting under a tree chatting and laughing. Lee was not among them. Janet became uneasy. What if Lee had gone off with a stranger? She had constantly told her to stay at the gate, no matter who told her that they were there to fetch her. She hoped that Lee had understood this and was perhaps dawdling in the classroom or toilet.

Her search proved fruitless. When questioned, the girls under the tree said that they thought they had seen Lee walking with a group of girls towards the bus stop. Janet was now frantic. Where had Lee gone? She had never been on a bus with anyone, ever. Janet rushed home and called all the people she thought Lee might have gone home with. When this also proved to be fruitless, she telephoned the police and gave them a description of her and the school uniform she was wearing. Three hours passed before the police finally traced Lee to the downtown bus terminal, where Janet found her sitting quietly on a chair in a bus company official's office. She did not appear to be upset or even aware of her predicament.

'I'm sorry, Mrs Jackson, I tried to find out where she was from or the name of her school, but she didn't seem to know either of them. She told me her name was Lee, but her surname seemed to elude her. I waited a while, hoping that she would come up with some more information about herself, but she clearly couldn't so I reported her presence to the police.'

'Thank you for taking care of her. Thank heavens she's safe. How did she get here?'

'A young girl from her school, who didn't actually know her, brought her in to us explaining that Lee had got onto the bus with them, but didn't seem to know where to go when she got off with them at the terminus. Unfortunately she left before I realised that your daughter was unable to provide us with any personal details.'

Lee sat silently throughout the short conversation, and then as Janet reached out to her both she and Janet burst into tears.

On the way home Janet questioned her.

'Lee, why didn't you wait for me at the gate like you always do?'

There was no answer, so Janet tried a different approach.

'Lee, where were you going on the bus?'

'Home.'

There was no point in going on with the questions. For Lee the incident was closed, she had answered the question, and the discussion was over. Janet was exhausted.

'I can only imagine that she thought that if she got onto the bus as the other children did, she would be taken home like they were being taken home.'

Edward de Bono would have been proud of Janet's next comment.

'I suppose one could look at it as a burst of initiative,' she said, trying to puzzle out Lee's thinking.

The incident highlighted the fact that it was impossible to predict this young child's behaviour, and that we would always need to be ready for the unexpected. From this nightmarish event, Janet's understanding of Lee expanded and she accepted that as anything was possible, she would always have to be one step ahead of her.

Lee appeared to be untouched by the fuss and concern that she had caused. She never spoke of it, although she promised not to get onto the bus again or to follow the other children home. Janet accepted her promise, but made sure that she was always waiting outside the school well before Lee was let out. Inexplicably, her teachers had failed to contact Janet about Lee's misadventure, or their lack of foresight at not phoning so she could collect her earlier. After making a formal complaint to a most apologetic headmistress about the lack of supervision, Janet realised that Lee's safety was not something that could easily be shared or taken for granted. Ever since then, Janet has always tracked Lee's whereabouts with radar precision.

Recently I asked Lee about the incident, and she immediately dismissed my question and refused to talk about it.

'I don't know what you want. You can ask my mother.'

<hr />

Now a pupil at a large senior school, Lee waits in the school grounds, and like all teenagers, complains if Janet is a minute late, after which her next question is: 'What's for lunch?'

'Salad.'

'And?'

'And nothing, you're supposed to be on a diet.'

'I know,' she sighed.

'It's a big salad with lots of things in it.'

'Okay, okay.'

On went the earphones and the Walkman, and the drive home was accompanied by her unabashed and moderately atonal singing to whatever cassette she was listening to.

One of the problems Lee has faced throughout her school years has been the constant lack of friends. The children in her classes have always been friendly but she, partly through shyness which can make her stammer, and partly because she is slower than they are, has been unable to secure a 'real friendship'.

Her best opportunities have been through the various special groups which she has joined. One of them, a social held twice weekly at the local church hall, provided the members, many with Down syndrome, with a warm, friendly interactive environment. Although there was approximately a ten year disparity within their various ages, this did not prove to be an inhibiting factor. The purpose was to enjoy the evening and this they did by dancing, playing air-hockey, parlour games and having snacks before going home. It was at these meetings that Lee became aware of the opposite sex and enjoyed dancing with the young boys there, especially those with Down syndrome.

A few of the group followed this up with dancing lessons, which have been only moderately successful for Lee. They all enjoyed the one-on-one ballroom-style close dancing, but Lee found the discipline of the regular step routines tiresome. She is a modern girl and does the Spice Girl dancing routines, which she executes off pat with verve and grace.

When these social evenings unfortunately came to an end, and new entertainment could not be found, Janet decided to organise her own. As these young people could not easily frequent the city's nightclubs, they needed a substitute venue where they could have dinner and then dance the night away. Janet organised a series of twice-yearly dinner dances, which were held at various upmarket hotels. They were impressive dress-up affairs, which were hugely successful. The young people came in their party clothes and energetically danced until midnight to the non-stop music of a succession of friendly disc jockeys. Four or five of these 'balls' were held, each more successful than the last.

It was at this time that Lee had her first encounter with youthful competition, which came in the form of 'another woman'. The boy she liked to dance with already shared a long-standing and delightfully close relationship with another girl who also had Down syndrome. The two of them, both a few years older than Lee, had been friends since they were at school together. No matter how hard Lee tried to gain the boy's interest, she failed, and he remained faithful to his long-time love. Disappointed, she finally wrote him off, although she was at a loss to understand why he would not switch his affections over to her because she fancied him.

His failure to comply contributed to the end of Lee's dancing lessons and she returned to the safety of dancing in front of the TV with the Spice Girls or to the video version of 'Grease'. Because Lee is extremely musical and rhythmical she has picked up the dance movements and the beat with ease. She dances with grace and fluidity, tossing her shiny dark hair, and snaking her arms through the air as she performs the various set routines. Dancing in her room has become one of the things she refers to as 'my stuff'. It is also good exercise.

'Lee, can I join in the dancing?'

'I don't think so.'

'Why not, I love dancing?'

Lee looked at me quizzically, shook her head, and with a big smile announced,

'You're too old, gran.'

'You're wrong, Lee, I'm young. I just look old.'

'You could have fooled me,' she laughed. We had a cuddle and I left her to it.

Lee does not have the model figure she admires as she flips through her magazines, but instead she is well-built and not as tall as she would like to be. However, though solid, she is not overweight. This is probably due to her general compliance with Janet's food intake guidelines and her unwavering faith in her mother's judgement. She seldom fusses or begs for what Janet has christened 'fat foods'.

However, weight is an ongoing problem for her, and she has shouldered some of this responsibility by being reasonably careful about what she eats, especially when she is at school or visiting and Janet is not with her. She is not naturally physically active, so her intake needs this constant monitoring.

After the original group of small children with Down syndrome disbanded, Lee's birthdays became successively more difficult to arrange, as the group had provided enough partygoers between them to make each child's birthday a success. They loved the presents, the balloons and the dressing up, but most of all they loved the food. Then as she became a little older, lunch at McDonald's or the Pizza Hut with a couple of willing classmates managed to fill the gap for a few years.

Lately, as Lee has matured and has seen her brothers enjoy going out for a family birthday dinner, she has elected to do the same. The thrill of choosing the restaurant and the type of food to be served is an important part of the celebration for her. So far she has consistently chosen her long-time favourite eating-out food, Chinese. Lee is a dab hand at managing chopsticks, which she does with surprisingly neat movements. Added to this outing, she still likes to follow the tradition of a birthday cake for afternoon tea at home, as well as a cake to take to school. A birthday is not the time to diet!

When other members of the family celebrate an event, Lee usually makes her own card for them, and on occasion an elaborately painted and decorated box or bottle to accompany it. Lately she has progressed from hand-drawn to computer-generated message-cum-letter cards which are equally delightful. Whereas her grammar has its own charm, it surely befuddles the language and spelling suggestions the computer dares to offer her. And as her sentiments are beyond reproach, she employs her usual aplomb and ignores them!

Getting new clothes has always been a big event in Lee's life. Like most females she enjoys leafing through and making choices from the racks of clothes. She holds up each piece under her chin as she measures its effect against herself. She adores black and bright colours, but also harbours a soft spot for pink. She has a strong colour sense and mixes and matches what she wears according to the whim of the day. Janet only interferes if the outfit is either too outrageous or not suited to the weather conditions. Her favourite fabrics are satin, velvet, lace and leather, rather typical teenage choices. Lee seldom reacts to cold weather and frequently under-dresses.

Walking through the Warehouse's clothing section during an afternoon shopping expedition, Lee fell in love with a bright pink feather boa which she joyously draped around her neck, letting it fall over her red T-shirt and blue denim jeans. No amount of persuasion could make her take it off. For Lee, the time and place she was in had disappeared. She had taken a leap into her imagination as she twirled and tossed the boa around herself. The look of ecstasy on her face gave Janet little option but to buy it for her.

Andy was born when Lee was almost three years old. It was her turn to feel displaced, yet somehow this never happened. For Lee, life carried on. At first she showed some interest in baby Andy, but as Janet was unsure of her possible reactions she was careful that Lee's time with him was well supervised. She let Lee sit on a chair and hold the baby in her lap, but always took him from her after a short while. Her biggest fear was that Lee might pick Andy up and simply dump him when she had had enough of him.

Last week Janet had to collect Andy from the city, and as she will not leave Lee at home alone I was called in to save the day, as she wanted to stay home and play her CDs. Janet is not happy about leaving Lee alone at home for more than ten to fifteen minutes at a time. Although she is eighteen years old, and keeps her mobile phone handy, her reactions remain unpredictable. Because of this it was decided that Janet would drop her off at my house, which she did, together with her CDs and half-eaten chicken pie, and the inevitable bottle of tomato sauce.

'Hurry up, Lee. Leave the tomato sauce. I'm sure Ma has some at her house.'

'And maybe she doesn't, then what?' answered Lee, already swaddling the bottle in several plastic bags to prevent it from leaking out onto her 'stuff'. She is well aware of the priorities in her life.

Now that Janet has started a course of evening art lessons, these visits have become a regular Wednesday evening outing for Lee. She arrives armed only with her pie, as she now trusts my ability to provide the tomato sauce to accompany it. Until David or Janet collect her, we spend the time watching 'soaps' on TV. Lee hogs the remote and blithely surfs the channels at great speed, paying little attention to the fact that she is not the only one watching. What is intriguing is that she is able to follow each fragment simultaneously, thereby seeing more than one programme at the same time. When she has had enough of this we have lovely uninterrupted one-on-one chats about 'life'.

Lee is most concerned about the fact that I do not have a husband, who she refers to as a 'man', and she makes the most hilarious choices on my behalf.

'Maybe I don't need to have a 'man' or a husband. What do you think about that, Lee?'

'It's not right.' She thought for a moment. 'Why don't you need one, Gran? My mother has one.'

'Yes, that's true she has, but perhaps I'm too busy.'

'I don't think so.'

'You can find me one if you like.'

'Oh, Gran, where will I do that?'

'I don't know, but it's you who wants me to have one.'

'Okay, okay, I'll do that.'

'Lee, how do you know what sort of person I need?'

'That's easy. He must be old and have white hair.'

'Do you really think I ought to be married, Lee?'

'Of course, but why ask me? Ask your daughter.'

Following her spontaneous bus trip from school to nowhere, her years at primary school were reasonably uneventful. Academically her progress was slow, and by the time she was ten she was still unable to read, although she was adept at recognising a simple story from following the pictures, and so gave the impression of reading. It was at this time that the family left South Africa for New Zealand.

Lee's life was about to take a dramatic leap forward.

PART TWO

MOVING TO
A NEW COUNTRY

The move went smoothly for Lee. She already had some experience of travel, having visited family in Australia, and she was excited about the trip. Where Janet went, Lee was happy to follow. However, she occasionally mentions some of the things she did together with her black nanny, Lenet, whom she loved and who carried her tied onto her back, African-style, when she was a baby. Lee spent many peaceful hours sleeping in the comforting warmth that flowed from Lenet's body as she worked around the house. The real benefit derived from these hours may never really be known or fully appreciated.

Her new school brought a change in Lee, which was noticeable by the end of her first term there. Although she had been the only child with Down syndrome at the school, the understanding, encouragement and support that she received there slowly enabled her budding personality to unfold, one petal at a time.

During the next few years Lee was still unable to make any friends at school. However, she did develop a loose contact with a young boy in the neighbourhood with whom she occasionally played, and who also had Down syndrome. And although she was unable to keep up with the children in her class, she benefited from the extra help given to her by her 'teacher aid' and was often rewarded with a certificate for trying or improving. These certificates, which were given out at the end of term, gave her a great deal of confidence and a sense of pride. However, she had not learnt to read by the time she left for secondary school.

Another big shift in her life occurred when she moved up into the senior school. The seeds of a new self-image began to break through. This was partly due to the acknowledgement and recognition given to her by the other children, which was a novel and enriching experience for her.

Her lack of approachability while she was at the junior school resulted in her eventually being somewhat sidelined. Now that she was getting sensitive, friendly and persistent attention from children who were her physical age and therefore old enough to understand her problems, it almost overwhelmed her. It took quite some while before she managed to overcome her shyness and respond to them, but their persistence won in the end. She was also getting older. The school staff arranged for some of the children to sit with her and include her in their lunch break. She began to feel as if she belonged. The sensitivity and care shown by the staff and children gradually established a place for her in the class, in the school and in the day.

At the beginning of her first year at secondary school, Lee was allocated a teacher aid, Kathy, with whom she slowly built up a strong personal relationship. Lee now fondly regards Kathy as a friend rather than as a teacher, confiding in her and chatting openly about her problems, her boyfriend and her family, as she might do with any girlfriend. At this point a chat with Kathy about their relationship and about Lee's progress at school seemed appropriate. We arranged to meet at a beachfront café.

'Kathy, would you tell me a little about Lee at school? We only know her at home and wonder what she's like at school.'

'Mmm, well, as you know, I've known Lee and worked with her now for about five years and we have built up quite an understanding between us.'

'Yes, I know. I also know that she is sufficiently confident and comfortable with you to be able to sleep over at your house. This is a huge step for her.'

'Yes, I realise that. She's quite a delightful visitor. She comes with a big bag packed full of her 'stuff' — Walkman, notebooks, pens and tapes, most of which she doesn't use because we are usually busy doing other things. I think it's just her comfort bag.'

'She brings all that 'stuff' to my house too. Come to think of it, Kathy, she seldom goes anywhere without carrying a bag of something.'

'Getting back to what you asked about her life at school. You probably know that she doesn't make friends easily. Anyway, if she does form a friendship, unless she gets the friend's undivided attention she drops her quite unceremoniously. She can't handle being in more than one relationship at a time.'

'Have you any idea why?'

'Not really, perhaps she's shy or suspicious. I'm not actually sure of the reason. Possibly it's just a lack of maturity, which she may overcome eventually.'

'Maybe, but from the young girls with Down's I've met, they all seem to be quite single-minded about their friendships. Do you think she enjoys being at school?'

'Yes I do, and she's extremely cooperative and willing to get involved in most of the things we do. You know, she is quite keen to learn. In fact, often when I look around to make sure that she gets off to the next lesson in another classroom, I find that she has already packed her things and gone ahead. The fact that she can now recognise most of the words she needs for the day to proceed smoothly means she's able to look up her timetable and get on with it. It's a big step up for her.'

'I know that Lee likes to have things in order, so a timetable is obviously important to her because it confirms what she enjoys most and that's having a set routine.'

Our coffee arrived, disrupting our conversation. As we sat drinking it, we watched the sun slide into a great flounce of puffy white clouds, instantly edging them with rose-gold tints. A reminder that time was passing and that Kathy would need to get home to her family. Smiling, she broke the silence.

'She's so much more confident and communicative in a chatty way than she was last year. I think that having a boyfriend has done a lot for her self-esteem.'

'No doubt the long phone calls she has with him have helped to relax some of the tension that seems to have held her back.'

'You know she has a huge sense of humour. If she is ever in doubt about doing something I ask her to do, she will respond very quickly if I turn it into a humorous approach. She's very playful.'

'What do you think about her 'work experience' efforts?'

'She takes working in the playschool with the toddlers very seriously, and is only too happy to cuddle and soothe the children. She's also very gentle with them. She is also a star at cleaning and tidying up before she leaves there.'

'Thanks, Kathy.'

'Before I finish, can I add something?'

'Sure.'

'I found it quite hard with Lee when I first started working with her. She was so unresponsive, but now she is contributing and giving so much that I really look forward to being at the school and working with her. We have a lot of fun and share a lot of laughs. She makes the work and the day worthwhile for me.'

One afternoon after school we were sitting on the settee enjoying the late afternoon sun as it filtered through the net curtain into the lounge. I decided to have a chat with Lee before she escaped into her bedroom world of music or TV — a world in which she has no 'people' pressure, where she can be in her own private reality without time constraints. She can switch and flick herself from one activity to another, dancing, dreaming and singing.

'How's school, Lee?'

'Not bad.'

'What did you do today?'

'Oh Gran, I did the usual.'

'Well, what was that?'

'Typing, drama and babies.'

'I've heard of typing and drama as subjects, but never babies.'

'You are funny, Gran. It's about how they get here.'

'Oh, and how's that?'

'Mum, tell your mother something.'

'She asked you, Lee.'

'I know she did, but you're the daughter, so tell her.'

From this I concluded that she somehow felt that the subject was taboo, and that she could not easily discuss it with me. How had the school presented it to the class? Since this information was not to come from Lee, I asked a couple of girls from her class how they had found the lesson. They seemed to be comfortable about discussing it, so I have to assume that Lee has some notion of her own about what is private and what is not. She was certainly aware of the concept, as a handwritten note suddenly appeared on her bedroom door: 'My room, my privacy'. It was no use knocking on the door for permission to enter, as it was impossible to knock loudly enough for her to hear anything above the volume of her music. Her request was tacitly understood.

Senior school and getting older is starting to have a positive effect on Lee's personality. As she accomplishes more, her self-confidence increases. She is more outgoing and contactable. After her first question (which has also become her traditional greeting), 'What's for lunch?' has been suitably answered by Janet as she gets into the car after school, she has started offering snippets of information about her day. Until now, it has been almost impossible to get any information from her about her school activities.

'I worked in the playschool today.'

'Doing what?'

'Making dough for the children. And I had to clean up.'

'Did you play with the dough?'

'Don't be silly, I made it.'

'Could you choose the colour?'

'I think so.'

'You can't think so if you've already done it.'

'Okay.'

'Okay what? So what colour did you choose?'

'Yellow and green.'

Lee began to stutter. She wanted to add something about the children, but seemed to be having difficulty organising her thoughts into words. I waited for her to continue.

'I asked her to sit on my lap, but she didn't stay for long.'

I assumed she meant one of the toddlers.

'That was sweet of you, Lee.'

'I know.'

Janet explains that this is one of the activities that have been offered to Lee in lieu of work experience. Her teacher has confirmed that she performs these tasks perfectly and seems to positively enjoy doing them. Taking advantage of what Janet calls one of Lee's 'high times', she decided that it might be an opportune moment to develop the conversation further.

'Would you like to work at that little school when you leave your school?'

'Maybe.'

Janet didn't get any further. It was clearly still difficult for Lee to make a firm commitment, whether positive or negative, so she returned to her old standby escape of 'maybe'. She shrugged and looked out the window. Clearly she did not want to get involved in discussing her future. Was it a question of being tired after a day at school, or was the concept of a working future too difficult for her to cope with? Because Lee usually switches off when she feels that the conversation has gone far enough, communication with her remains fragmentary.

These short attention spans make any in-depth continuity extremely difficult to pursue, and her rebuffs are stubbornly final for the encounter of the moment. However, it is possible to reintroduce a previously discussed subject after a suitable time lapse, which could be at least a week or more. An alternate approach to the subject using a different angle, or a playful humorous entry, can catch her interest and obtain a response.

As Lee has become more adept at writing, she has begun to write short notes to Janet on a variety of subjects. Janet keeps a small pad on the kitchen bench on which the family jots down the items they want her to add to the grocery list. Lee began her note-writing by adding to this. Her requests are usually reasonable and practical, and she would add things like 'tomato saws' well before her beloved sauce bottle was empty. These are the little things from which we read her developmental processes. Her note has indicated that she is able to plan ahead. Of course, she may have been thinking and planning ahead well before this, but it was never evident.

Picking up these clues is like doing detective work. Her developing self-confidence and ability to write is allowing us to extend our understanding of her thought processes. She is not averse to pinning her handwritten notices onto the refrigerator door, warning her brothers not to eat her frozen orange juice lollies. Her bedroom door has also not escaped her notes, the most frequent being about her privacy.

'My privacy. Private Private Private – not coming in.'

She has recently started talking and writing about the dreams she has, many of which are related to 'love'. Here is a delightful example of a note about a dream:

'Mum, I dromd about the boy at my school he did like me he did haug (hug) me he was going to kiss me.'

She was unable to elaborate verbally on the dream.

'You can read my letter to my mother.'

Lee was 'in love'. It was not difficult to find out exactly who the object of her delight was, because pictures of him began to appear all over her bedroom wall. Cut-outs of her beloved TV star, John Stamos, now smile down at her from every published photographic angle. He has become a galaxy all on his own. Lee has searched, found and bookmarked several promising sites on him on the internet. These she visits non-stop. Printing photographs of John Stamos has become a full-time occupation for her. She writes long love letters to him, in which she freely expresses her dislike for his wife. She is following the pattern of any young girl in her early teens who is 'crazy' about a film or pop star, except that for Lee it has come about three years later. Unfortunately, this crush is preventing her from forming a close relationship with one of the boys she knows, who also has Downs syndrome. She is full of expectations as to the qualities of her ideal man.

'Gran, he must be tall and dark and handsome.'

'Like John Stamos?'

'What do you think!'

At this point I began to wonder what she was thinking.

'Lee, do you know what love is?'

'Well, there's a man and a woman and they love each other, then they get married and have some kids, and that's it,' she finished triumphantly.

The advent of her school prom has provided a dilemma, which she has animatedly and endlessly debated with Janet. Who should she invite to partner her? She knew which of the Down's boys were the best dancers, having frequently danced with them at parties. She decided to ask Danny. Although he is quite a few years older than Lee, they have enough in common not to let their age difference deter them.

'Lee,' I asked, 'why Danny?'

'I don't know.'

'That's not an answer, Lee. You chose him, you must know why.'

'Well.'

'Yes?'

'Well, he's asked me to be his girlfriend.'

'Oh, when did he do that?'

Lee started to stutter and blush.

'On the phone, and he says he has a dress suit so it will be easy for him to come along.'

'Is he the one who kissed you goodbye the other day?'

'Grannn!'

'Well is he?'

'Yes, I suppose so.'

I pushed it a bit further.

'Is he a good kisser?'

'Ma, listen to what your mother is saying.'

No answer from Janet.

'Gran, what can I say… yes.'

'Then that seals it, he's obviously the right one for the dance.'

Lee was getting embarrassed, so I changed direction.

'What about a dress for the prom?'

'Ask Janet, my mother.'

'No, Lee, I'm asking you. What sort of dress do you fancy?'

'I told you. Ask my mother.'

I was not going to get any satisfaction from Lee, who clearly had every confidence in Janet's choice. This was never going to be an easy matter, as Lee's figure does not fit the conventional sizing of most clothes, especially dresses, so the hunt began early. After trying what seemed like all the girls' shops in Auckland, Janet decided to have something made up for her. She would find a lovely top and have the skirt made to go with it.

Like many children who have Down syndrome, Lee has sensitive skin, so the material and how the seams are finished have to be taken into account. This made trimmings and sequins almost off limits, until Janet found a beautifully beaded satin top in a shop that specialises in Indian saris. She then had a tailor cut out and sew the skirt to Lee's measurements. She looked dazzling, her dark hair and creamy skin looked radiant in the harmonious tones of her fuchsia satin ensemble.

On the afternoon of the dance Janet took Lee to the hairdresser, an outing she always enjoys. She was amazingly composed as she spent the rest of the afternoon in her room doing her usual activities. However, she let her excitement show by promptly answering Janet's call to her to get into the shower. Normally she would need to be called several times.

Lee eventually emerged from her room as if walking on air. She moved with the grace of one who knows that she is lovely, and she was. Without any help from Janet, Lee had made up her own face with a light touch of perfectly applied make-up. She was ready for her first prom.

On the way to fetch Danny, Janet brought her past my house so that I could see Lee in her finery. I was waiting outside in the cold with my flash-ready camera. Lee posed in the driveway, happily oblivious to the freezing weather.

The dance was all she had hoped for, and Danny, who looked appropriately smart in his black dress suit, proved to be the right choice of partner. Lee came home clutching a photograph of Danny and herself, which now has a permanent position on the mantle shelf in the sitting room. So far Danny has not qualified for a position on Lee's bedroom wall with John Stamos.

'How was the dance, Lee?'

'Okay.'

She blushed and walked away.

It's quite clear that they both enjoyed their evening together, as they have started making telephone calls to each other.

Finding dresses for Lee is not the only shopping difficulty regarding her clothes. Much more problematic is locating shoes that fit. The chubby width of her feet makes them too large for children's fittings and too small for adult sizes. They may, quite delightfully, have been designed by Lucy Attwell. Fortunately, Lee is not too fussy about the style, although she sighs for a pair of Spice Girl platforms. Being desperate, Janet has tried having shoes made for her, but these lie unworn in Lee's cupboard. They are too 'heavy', and the homemade seams are too bulky and irritate her sensitive skin. Janet is constantly on the lookout for suitable wide, low-cut shoes of any colour or make, and generally pops into every new shoe shop she comes across. Meanwhile Lee is content to wear her soft, falling-apart old sandals and sneakers. She is confident that Janet will provide the right shoes when needed.

Lee has never doubted that Janet can fix or put right any difficulty that she may find herself in at any time. Although this faith in Janet has provided Lee with a strong sense of security, it is a daunting responsibility for a mother who knows that one day she will not be around for her daughter to lean on. It is possible that Lee may one day leave home and work at some sheltered type of employment and live in a group with a bunch of other people with Down syndrome, but that still seems to be a long way off.

Lee has occasional short snatches of intimacy with her brothers. Their relationship with her is mainly protective. Frequently, they playfully challenge her, trying to rouse her into more than a casual response. Andy, who is almost three years younger than Lee, has the most difficult task regarding his relationship with her. Lee sees him as a problem, because when they first arrived in New Zealand they shared a bedroom, and from this she has retained the notion that he is somewhat invasive. Being eight years old at that stage, he allowed himself the freedom of coming in and out of their room whenever he wanted to. Lee does not easily give up things that she has once latched onto and Andy's license and indeed his rights at that time were not easily tolerated.

Although they are going through a period of little contact right now, Andy is always willing to stay and 'babysit' her in the house when Janet asks him to. They just do not chat together. However hard Andy tries, Lee makes a good job of ignoring him after dismissing him with a monosyllabic reply.

Jake, being much older than Lee, has always had the advantage of being more aware of her needs and frequently takes her out for a meal or to a movie. She enjoys these outings and regards them as a sort of date. He has also had some enchanting conversations with her.

'What did you do at school today, Lee?'

She looked up into his face, surprised by the question.

'Why do you want to know?'

'Ah, I was just asking if you'd had a good day.'

'It was okay.' Lee made herself comfortable on the settee opposite him. 'A boy opened the door for me to go through.'

'That was nice. What did you say to him?'

'I just said, "thank you".'

Knowing that Lee had recently been to a movie with Danny, Jake chatted on.

'I believe you went on a date.'

Becoming embarrassed, she did not answer.

'Who did you go with?' Jake asked casually.

'A boy.'

'I know that, but who was he?' he laughed encouragingly.

'Just a boy.'

'Lee, I want to know something about him. We tell you about our girlfriends.'

'I know. He's a boy, Down's like me, and we went to a movie.'

'And then?'

Laughter and blushes.

'And then?' he pressed her further.

'I walked with him, his name is Danny, to his front door and we kissed.'

'What! Kissed?' he teased.

'Well, so what — we kissed, that's all.'

The game was on.

'Who kissed who?'

'On my lips.'

'Wow!'

Jake felt that he may have gone far enough and was not about to pressure her further. However, she felt that his response required one from her.

'We didn't do sex or anything, so don't ask me.'

The date Jake had referred to was an afternoon movie followed by burgers at McDonald's. Because Danny is not in possession of a driver's licence, Janet performs the taxi duty, after which he is always dropped off at his house. This necessitates the walk up his driveway and a front door goodbye kiss.

It was a warm summer afternoon and Janet dropped the 'couple' near the cinema, and watched as they walked arm in arm past the shops and into the theatre. Lee, with her cell phone primed in case of an emergency, was instructed to call Janet once they had eaten their after-movie burgers. They were to wait outside McDonald's to be picked up. Panic set in as our eyes swept past the entrance of the burger house and they were nowhere to be seen. We decided to drive around the block once more in case they had gone back into the shop for something. As we approached the first corner we found them sitting on a bench holding hands, laughing and chatting as they waited for us.

After walking Danny to his door, Lee returned to the car smiling broadly. Affectedly she tossed her shiny black hair over her shoulder as she approached us, but before getting into the car Lee bent down and, presenting her flushed smile-crinkled face at the open front window, made her big announcement.

'I'm in love.' She looked quite beautiful as she blushed to a deeper pink.

Once in the car, she sighed. She was ready to chat. Janet asked the crucial question.

'Did you kiss Danny goodbye?'

'Of course, and I'm definitely in love.'

We all made sounds of approval as we happily broke into laughter. Lee laughed with us, but quite suddenly her mood changed. The pinnacle of her day had slipped into an anti-climax, and she lashed out at Janet, ordering her not to laugh. She became serious and withdrawn. Her mother tried to lift her by explaining that she had just come from having a lovely day and that they would do it again. Lee responded grudgingly.

'Okay.'

We drove on silently for a while, but it was clear that Lee was becoming depressed. I tried to chat with her.

'Are you all right, Lee?'

'I'm thinking.'

'Oh, okay.' I waited for a while before I continued, hoping to break her mood.

'Lee, may I ask for our book, when you say you are thinking what are you actually thinking about?'

I waited, but no answer came. I knew when I was beaten.

Thinking was a subject we had never discussed. What was her concept of thinking? What did she mean when she said she was thinking and what sort of things did she think about? A few days later she was standing in front of her mirror brushing her hair and listening to the radio. She did not hear me come in, but as she saw my reflection in the mirror she switched off the radio but continued to brush her hair.

'Your hair looks so shiny, Lee. Do you brush it often?'

'Not really.' She waited to see what my next move would be, but I continued to watch her without speaking. She became embarrassed, then turning towards me asked. 'What do you want?'

'Nothing, I just thought we could talk.'

'About what?'

'Something for our book.'

Lee's interest in the book was fading. However, when asked something directly about it she livens up and becomes more than willing to make a contribution towards it.

'Like what?'

'Perhaps about thinking. I was wondering what you think about?'

'Well Gran, I'm thinking now,' she paused, letting a playful smile flicker across her face. 'I think about things that happen on TV and at my school.'

This was a reasonable and in some ways an informative answer. That she gave time to replaying events that she had experienced added another tiny bit of the puzzle to the whole picture. Because she does not discuss much of her life with us, it is extremely difficult to know the extent or the effect an experience, however small, may have on her.

That she can and does mull over things in which she has been involved must add a dimension to the experience and to her life. Perhaps her thoughts are richer and deeper and more rewarding than she can express, or than we can understand, and that she is therefore able to get more from life than just passing through a day of events.

On the surface Lee appears to be a contented young girl, and it is only on intermittent occasions that she becomes depressed and distant. Like most teenagers she wants time for herself, and frequently turns down an opportunity to go out. Instead she prefers to stay in her room doing her 'stuff', which now includes writing in her journal and writing love letters to John Stamos. So far Danny has not been able to replace him.

'Lee, do you want to write about the music you like?'

'Could be.'

'So what do you want to say?'

'Well, you know I like the Spice Girls.'

'Yes, I do.'

'Then you can write about that if you like.'

'It's not if I like, Lee. I thought you were to share writing this story with me.'

'I am.'

'Oh, how do you make that out?'

'We're talking about it right now.'

'Yes, but that's not writing about it.'

'So, Gran, I am telling you and you can write it down.'

'Don't you want to write it yourself?'

'Not now.'

'Should we leave it to another time?'

'If you like.'

'Okay, but if I do, can I be sure you'll write it then?'

'Maybe.'

She hesitated, waiting for my next move. The moment could not be wasted.

'Lee, let's pretend that this is an interview, so find something to use as a microphone.'

This activity, if we could get it going, would prevent her from sliding into a day of isolation in her room. She liked the idea and went off in search of a 'microphone'. I heard her rummaging through an eclectic collection of items housed in a large wooden Pandora's box that she kept under her bed.

This search must have proved futile, because the next thing I heard was the snapping open and shut of a number of kitchen cupboard doors. A few minutes later she returned with two empty ice-cream cones, one of which she handed to me. Ice-cream cone microphone in hand, I asked a serious-looking Lee our first question.

'Good morning, Lee. I'm going to ask you some questions about yourself. Is that okay?'

'Of course.'

'Right. Let's start with your age. How old are you?'

'You know that.'

'Yes I do, but it's an interview question.' She screwed up her mouth, then waved her hand at me indicating that I should continue. 'So Lee, how old are you?'

'I'm eighteen. Soon.'

'Right. I know that you're at senior school, so I want to ask you about it. Do you have many friends there?'

'Not really.'

'Are the children there not friendly or something?'

'No, they're okay, but they aren't my friends. I think it's because I'm Down's.'

I felt as if I had been slapped, but realised that I needed to respond quickly.

'I don't think that's the reason. Perhaps it's because you aren't friendly towards them. What about that for a reason?'

Lee had not displayed any emotion when she had answered. For her it was the reason and a fact.

'Well, I'm waiting?'

'Maybe,' she conceded.

We may both have been right, but not wanting to pursue that line further, I changed the subject.

'Who do you phone the most often?'

'My cousins in Australia.'

'What do you talk about?'

'Stuff. So many questions, Gran.'

'Yes, that's what an interview is all about.'

'I know that.'

'Right. Next question, are you ready?'

'You know I am.' Lee laughed, and looking up into Janet's face asked her playfully, 'What's the matter with your mother? Do something with her.'

'What do you want me to do?' Janet asked just as playfully as she walked by.

'Anything,' Lee called out after her.

'Come on Lee, this is a serious interview and I'm waiting to continue.'

'I know that.'

Lee was now one big cuddly giggle. But the moment was lost. Her attention span had run out.

I still wanted to follow up on the phone calls, because I had heard her complain to Janet that unlike the other members of the family who always seem to be talking on the phone, no one ever phoned her. I tried again.

'Why don't you ever phone me, Lee?'

'I've got nothing to say.'

'Nonsense, you've always got plenty to say.'

'Like what?'

'To start with you should realise that if you don't phone people then they won't phone you back.'

'And?'

'You got me, Lee, I'm getting tired. What about you?'

'Yes me too, so can we eat the cones?'

After slowly demolishing her cone, Lee became relaxed and chatty.

'I will write something now, Gran.'

'Great, what do you want to write about?'

'I'm not sure.'

Lee turned to face Janet, who had come back into the room and was now sitting on the settee beside her. Like a young puppy she snuggled onto her lap. Janet gave her a long hug, then extricating herself from under Lee's not too puppy-like weight she got up and went into the kitchen. Lee became quiet, pensive even, and then quite suddenly she called out a stunningly unexpected question.

'Mum, what did you think when I was born and you saw that I was Down's?'

Janet caught her breath and, not looking up from the kettle she was filling, was clearly trying to prepare her reply. To give Janet more time to consider her answer, I interjected.

'Is that what you want to write about, Lee?'

'Maybe.' She turned back to Janet waiting for her to respond.

'I was pleased to see you.'

'That's not what I asked you.'

'As I said, I was pleased to see you. You were such a pretty little bundle and, what's more, I'm still pleased to see you.'

Lee, half-satisfied with Janet's answer, gave up and turned to me.

'I'm ready, Gran. What shall I write about?'

'There are lots of things people could be interested in, like what you want to do when you leave school, and what your interests are — besides boys, that is.'

Lee blushed, and then became serious.

'Okay.'

'I'm ready, Lee.'

'Well. He must be tall and handsome.'

'Just a minute, Lee, who must be tall and handsome?'

'Gran, we're talking about when I get married.'

'Right, go on.'

'As I said, he must be tall and handsome and not Down's. And I will look after the baby.'

Lee is sure that one day she will be married, and although she does not have a timeframe for this, it remains an unshakable concept. Many of her ideas of marriage have come from the various soaps she watches on TV. She has mixed these in with the home life around her. Notwithstanding this blend, she sees married life in fairly simple terms. Her husband would go to work every day while she stayed at home. When the need arose he would take her shopping for food, and then help carry the bags into the house.

'I will make the meals and look after the baby.'

'You won't be working then?'

'No, Gran, you're not listening. I can't work when I am looking after the baby.'

'Sorry, carry on.' I had upset her train of thought and she began to stutter, so I went on. 'Lee, just a minute, do you mean that he will provide all the money for you and the baby?'

'Now you've got it. And he will also get some money from the bank.'

'Just like that.'

'Ma, your mother doesn't know much about the bank!'

She gave me a look of disdain before answering my question as to how she would look after the baby.

'I know what to do. I will feed it and teach it to talk and to walk.'

'Lee, I hope you don't mind this question, but as your gran I need to know that you know.'

'Know what?'

'How the baby gets made?'

Lee dropped her eyes and once again she blushed, the uprush of colour invading every dimple and crease that surrounded her shy smile.

'Gran, how can you ask me that!'

'Before girls get married parents always check this out.'

'Oh. They told us at school. It's disgusting.'

'Well it's not disgusting if you're married.'

'Maybe. Anyway, I don't know who the man is that I'm going to marry yet.'

Lee went on to describe the 'big' white dress she would wear for the wedding which she confidently expects Janet will choose and buy for her.

Lee invokes so much tenderness with the revelations she makes without uttering a word. Her face reveals all her thoughts immediately and expressively as they arrive. She so easily becomes awash with vulnerable expressions of innocence. At times her lack of comprehension not only increases her vulnerability, it also denies her any form of emotional protection.

This was the first time that we had gone into detail about her expectations of life after school. So far, she has not expressed an interest in a specific type of work, but has accepted the fact that she will work before she gets married. She remains lukewarm about working in the crèche and half supports an idea of working in a shop.

She thoroughly enjoyed tidying and packing shelves at the New World supermarket during a spell of work experience organised by her school. Now, when out grocery shopping with Janet, she cannot resist straightening items on the shelves as she walks along the aisles. Because she knows which items Janet usually buys, she is a great help with the shopping and gathers the regulars into the shopping trolley before her mother asks for them or perhaps even needs them.

Along the way she adds the odd bag of dried apple rings, a smoothie or other snack she fancies. She often adds a packet of biscuits 'for Gran's tea'. When Janet goes through the trolley removing the 'excess items', Lee becomes quite rattled, explaining in no uncertain terms exactly why she needs them. However, her objections are short-lived, and she concedes defeat by accepting one of the selected items as her prize. Her spirits are further lifted as she meticulously replaces the items in their correct positions on the shelves.

'Lee, one day when we were chatting, you told me that maybe you wanted to work in a shop.'

'So?'

'Do you still want to do that?'

'You can ask my mother. I heard my mum speak to my teacher about that I can go to college and about which one.'

'Oh, what would you do there that would make it easy for you to get a job afterwards?'

'Well, I do English and French and typing.'

'What job could you do with that?'

'If they say I must go somewhere, I will go there.' Lee raised her eyes. 'I can act.'

This new interest is the result of the recent introduction of drama classes to her curriculum.

'Would you really do it?'

'Of course. The lady or the man will show me and I can do it.'

'I suppose I will just have to wait until I see you on TV.'

'Oh, Gran!'

'By the way, can I have that picture of you smiling to use in our book?'

'I don't know how many we have got.'

'Oh that doesn't matter. I can have some copies made.'

'Then that's okay.'

Lee has days of great exuberance, just as she has days of quiet unapproachable introversion. After charting these days on the calendar there still doesn't appear to be an explanation for this. They are not related to her menstrual cycle, which she hates and is convinced is unnecessary.

'People should not have to do this,' she told Janet when she had her first period. I had wondered how she would handle these times of the month, but I need not have worried. She has accepted it and takes it in her stride, mood swings and all. However, her opinion of it has not changed.

Lee has always been a quiet person, not trying very hard to express herself, but shortly after her seventeenth birthday all that changed. And a glorious period of verbalisation, which has been an absolute revelation, has ensued. It's possible, or reasonable, to assume that she may have harboured many opinions and ideas before but has not had the need, or perhaps the vocabulary, to express them. Her new-found 'voice' has allowed her a more prominent interaction with those around her. She has begun to tease, to pun and to joke. She catches on more quickly and has a quirky sense of humour. She has entered a new age of self-confidence.

Recently, the teacher informed Janet that a young girl in Lee's class at school had died, and would she please explain this to her at the appropriate moment. I asked Janet if Lee understood the concept of death and how she had taken it.

'Oh yes, she understands it all right, and has spoken to me about her fear of death and of dying.'

'When and how did you broach the subject?'

'One day she asked me why she didn't have a sister like I have. I explained that long ago, before she was born, I had a baby girl called Sally who had not lived very long after her birth.'

'Did she follow this easily?'

'Yes, but she was more intrigued by the fact that she'd had a sister than that she had died. However, because she wanted to know where Sally had gone to, this proved to be a good way to introduce and discuss the fact that people die.'

'It must have still been difficult to explain.'

'Not really, because she could see that Sally was not around, so she understood that she was gone and dying meant that the person was gone. But she surprised me somewhat by saying that she was afraid of dying too. Don't forget that she sees people dying on TV and in films, so she understands the idea quite well.'

'In that respect, TV had and is still a strong influence in her learning process.'

'It certainly is,' Janet called over her shoulder as she opened the door to let the cat in.

'For instance,' she continued, as she settled into her chair again, 'she was very upset when Nicole Kidman died in the film 'Moulin Rouge'. But she also understood that it was only a film, and that she was acting, and that she was not really dead.'

'How do you think she grasped that?'

'Drama classes at school means she knows what acting is.'

'You never know where or what she picks up, or where it can lead.'

'That's why I think it's so important to expose her to as much wide and varied experience as we can.'

This seemed like an appropriate time to talk about religion and God.

'Lee, do you know what is meant by religion?'

'Not really.'

'Do you want to know?'

'I don't think so.'

'Any good reason why not?'

'Please, Gran.' Lee was becoming frustrated.

'Okay, but tell me Lee, do you know who God is?'

'Of course I do, but I don't know his name. I think he's just an old man.'

'Old like me?' She ignored this remark.

'I guess he's clever.'

'Do you know that he makes the day and the night happen?'

'My mum didn't tell me about that.'

'Why do you think he made the day and the night for us?'

'I told you, because he's clever and because some people are tired.'

'If you had to speak to him, what would you say?'

'I'd tell him something interesting.'

'Would you ask him why the sea had so much water in it?'

'No, I know that, it comes from all the rain that comes down. Also it's so that people can swim in the sea.'

Lee considered this for a moment. Then she gave me a big dismissive smile and the conversation was over. Religion, God and the universe still had some investigative potential, but they would have to wait their turn.

<hr />

September the 11th did not pass Lee by. She had watched the TV replay of this terrible event unfold. From the dismay and horror all around her she understood that this was news, that it was really happening, and that it was not a movie. After that day, wherever she was in the house, she dropped whatever she was doing and came running to the big TV if she heard the name Osama bin Laden or the "twin towers" mentioned.

'Lee, do you know who Osama bin Laden is?'

'I'm not really sure.'

'Have you seen him on TV?'

'Yes.'

'What does he look like?'

'He's really skinny and he has some beard. He's just talking to someone.'

'Is he a good man?'

'No!' her response was fast and emphatic.

'Do you know why they are looking for him?'

'Of course. I saw a big building and a plane, and a plane went into the side, and there was a lot of smoke, and people lost their jobs, and they were running and crying, and some died and they fell out.'

'Do you think they'll catch him?'

'The Americans have an army and they will fight and try to catch him when they can.'

'If they catch him what should they do to him?'

'The American army must kill his friends and catch him till he dies.'

'Yes. It's still so sad about the people in the buildings.'

For a moment Lee shut her eyes, and it was if she was replaying the event in her mind.

'Some of the people in the tower died and then fell out.'

'Did you see this all happen on TV?'

'I just saw it once and I don't want to see it again, that's my point.'

Since we had this conversation, Lee has not initiated any further discussion on this subject. However, if she hears Osama bin Laden's name mentioned on the media she invariably asks, 'Did they catch him?'

We were not left in any doubt as to her awareness of the difference between what is real and what is acting. It happened and she has let go of it. She does not link it to any threat to her own or to world security.

'Gran?'

'Yes.'

'Have we finished the book yet?'

'That depends on whether you want me to stop.'

'No it's okay. Did you tell them that I'm Down's?'

'Yes, is it okay?'

'Yes … do you think they'll mind?'

'Why should they mind?'

'I don't know. Will I stop being Down's?'

'I don't think so. Why would you want to stop being Down's, you're perfect just as you are?'

'I don't think so.'

'Lee, John Stamos would love you just as you are.'

'I hope so. What about Rebecca?'

'He can still love you even though he's married to Rebecca. One day you will fall in love with a 'real' person. Anyway, I thought you said that you were in love with Danny.'

'Oh Gran, don't you know anything, John Stamos is real.' Lee completely ignored the reference to Danny. For the moment, her mind was fixed on the thought process we were following.

'I know he's real, but I mean that one day the person you really fall in love with will be someone who is not a film star and who does not live so far away from here.'

'I will go to America, so then I can see him.'

'Perhaps.'

Because Lee has frequently travelled between South Africa, Australia and New Zealand and has made numerous national trips by plane, she is convinced that going to the USA is more than possible. Because of this her dream of meeting John Stamos lives on. She never refers to him as John — he is always accorded his full name.

<hr />

Lee is clearly deeply concerned about having Down syndrome and being different from the majority of people around her. When she was sixteen she was asked by Kathy, her teacher aid, during a casual conversation if she knew that she had Down syndrome. She answered without hesitation.

'Yes, of course.'

'What's it like having Down's?' her teacher asked.

'It's very hard.'

For a second, Kathy was stunned and unable to comment further. She had not expected such a fast or forceful answer. They discussed the subject a little further before they were both satisfied that they were ready for something else to talk about. Lee continued her day at school as usual and did not refer to their chat again. It is almost as if having had her say she let go and became objective and ready for the next item of the day. Her burst of emotion had simply been a sudden vehement outpouring, and then it was gone.

This was the first time that any of us had ever heard her thoughts on having Down syndrome. At first we were shocked, then surprised, as we had no idea that she was not only aware of her situation but that she was so clearly unhappy with it. It had never occurred to us to ask her. Since that day she has revived the subject at odd intervals. We do not dwell on it, or initiate it, or specifically raise it for discussion, but we do try to answer her questions as they arise. It is not a taboo subject, we just leave it to her to speak about it, if and when she feels so inclined.

We usually comment on the presence of another child or young adult with Down syndrome whom we may meet or pass in the street. She often makes the first comment, but is generally not interested beyond that. She is extremely conscious of having Down syndrome in the presence of the opposite sex. If a young boy or man of any age catches her eye and smiles at her as we are out walking, she blushes and comments how surprised she is that she has been acknowledged, particularly since she has Down syndrome.

Until we were given Lee, I was one of those people who purposely avoided eye contact with handicapped or disabled people. I had the idea that I would embarrass them by acknowledging them, that they may think that I was looking at them. Lee has made me realise that it is possible that handicapped people may wish to receive a simple act of recognition, of inclusion, so that they too can feel a part of society.

When Janet walked into her room, Lee was sitting quietly at her desk, copying dialogue from a paperback novel into her journal. She spoke without looking up.

'Mum, why am I white?'

'Well, because I'm your mother and I'm white.'

'Yes, but I can see that you're not Down's.'

'That's true.'

Lee nodded in agreement. She had made her point, but was not convinced that her challenge had been met. She put down her pen and, looking at Janet, fired her arrow.

'You wouldn't like to be Down's, would you?'

Although Janet was becoming used to these questions, they remained surprising and painful when they came. She answered teasingly.

'I wouldn't mind if I was as nice as you are.'

Overcome with frustration, Lee gave the most unexpected reply.

'Oh Mother, how bizarre!'

For a while Lee remained occupied by this thread of thought. One of the things that she particularly hates about having Down syndrome is being different from other people, so it was not too surprising when one day she turned to me with the following comment. We were sitting in Janet's car waiting for Andy, who needed a lift to his friend's house. Watching an animated conversation between Janet and myself, Lee, feeling chatty, joined in.

'Gran, you and my mother look the same.'

'You mean we look alike. That's because I'm her mother and she's my daughter.'

'I know that, but I'm her daughter, you know. She's my mother and we don't look alike.' She stopped for breath. 'I think that's because I'm Down's.'

'Lee, you do look a bit alike. You both have dark hair and brown eyes and your little nose is the best in the world.'

Lee sat quietly for a while, clearly mulling over my reply. Her answer to me was related, but a little removed and rather sad.

'At school a boy smiled at me, even though he knew that I'm Down's.'

Lee cannot see any acceptable reason for having Down syndrome. She is deeply hurt by it and it surfaces every so often. She thinks that having Down syndrome is to be inferior. It is not unreasonable that she should feel slighted, because generally people do not acknowledge or include her during conversations or small talk chatter. These unintentional exclusions exacerbate her feeling of inferiority.

It would not be helpful to try and explain that she is not included because she has Down syndrome, but it could simply be because some people are insensitive or do not have very good manners. It could be that perhaps they do not 'see' her, or that they are unsure of how to make contact with her, or what her response might be. It might also be that they are simply shy. To try to explain any of this runs the risk of confirming for her that she is indeed different. Being respected as a person is an unspoken but deeply understood priority of hers.

'Lee you are going to go deaf if you don't turn the music down,' Janet shouted from the doorway as she entered her room. Lee turned the player off.

'What do you want? I'm busy.'

'That's better, but you are also not being very nice. What are you busy doing? You just seem to be dancing.'

'That's what I'm saying, I'm busy. I don't know why you can't understand.'

'I do, but I'm worried about your hearing. Why are you so grumpy?'

Lee disregarded Janet's question.

'Don't be, I can hear everything. Now can I turn it on?'

She did and it was as loud as ever. Instead of being irritated by Lee's grouchiness and her lack of success in getting her to turn the radio down, Janet was delighted with the bit of rebellion that she was displaying. It brought her closer to the normal behaviour of any other teenager. Lee tends not to display any anger, instead either dismissing or ignoring whatever it is that she is confronting.

What would reasonably frustrate most parents who are trying to come to terms with their teenage daughter's behaviour thrills Janet.

It poses the question as to exactly how much of this teen behaviour is possibly ingested from their peers. Lee has minimal contact with her peers, yet she seems to be following their teen patterns of behaviour, even though it is occurring in her about four years later than expected.

It is also a possibility that she may be absorbing some teenage behavioural patterns from the various TV programmes she watches. Those she chooses to watch run stories that rely on various aspects of family relationships, or they lean heavily on romantic intrigue. Both types of programme provide her with hours of entry into their lives. She tapes the episodes, then sees them again and again, giving them her full attention as she simultaneously mouths the words as the stars speak them. She lives their lives.

When they go to the movies, Janet chooses films she knows that Lee will be able to follow without difficulty. They mainly need to have relatively uncomplicated dialogue. The amount and type of violence is also a point that has to be considered as Lee is easily affected and scared by harsh visual material.

She enjoys those films that feature the music she relates to. But there is no doubt that love stories remain her favourite. She happily enjoys seeing the films she likes over and over again. Some of her special repeats are 'Grease', 'Moulin Rouge' and 'Dirty Dancing'.

Janet takes her to live shows, like Robbie Williams and the Cirque de Soleil, which have been placed mid-way on her list of special favourites. However, after going to these shows she seldom, if ever, mentions either performance unless specifically asked about them. This seeming lack of recall may not necessarily mean that her memory is at fault. It is quite likely that her interests have shifted, and that she would rather concentrate on those of the moment.

<hr />

For Lee, Saturday night, usually the highlight of a teenager's week, was coming and going with uneventful regularity. She was not being invited out and was becoming acutely aware that she was on the outside looking in. She felt the buzz as her brothers made and received numerous phone calls as they sorted out their Saturday night entertainment with their friends.

To this she added the understanding she had gathered from her TV soaps that the weekend was party time. She began to loll around the house restlessly complaining that she was bored. Janet knew that Lee could so easily sink into herself, and as she described it 'blob out' in her room, so she created what was to become a regular event for them – Girls' Night.

Girls' Night is a Janet and Lee exclusive. It all started on a Saturday afternoon when the two of them went to the supermarket to buy the party 'nosh' — popcorn, dried fruit, juice and a special lolly treat for each of them. Lee entered into the spirit of the approaching evening the moment they pushed the trolley through the automatic doors of the supermarket.

She loved selecting the party food. As Janet collected the regular groceries, Lee, clutching a green plastic basket, would disappear into the maize of aisles to select her bounty. She would then return some minutes later and proceed to empty her prizes, one at a time into Janet's trolley, with far more deference than they warranted. At this point Janet generally had to move into damage control.

'I got you your dark chocolate, Mum,' Lee announced, holding up a 300g slab for her to see.

'Thanks, Lee, but would you change it for a smaller one please?'

Lee gave an impatient click, followed by a big cajoling smile.

'This is a good one, Mum. I can see it's okay.'

'Oh it's good all right, it's even too good!' Janet answered laughing. 'Please, Lee, change it. I don't want to get fat.'

With a slight shrug, Lee acquiesced and vanished into the confectionery section, deferentially holding the big chocolate with both hands. Chocolate was not to be trifled with.

'Here,' Lee said disdainfully as she placed a smaller one in the trolley.

'I think we've got everything. We can put this all in the car and come back to the video shop.'

'You have to pay.'

'I will. Come on, let's go before you find something else we need.'

It did not take long to choose a video. If they could not find one that they had not seen, Lee was perfectly content to hire and re-watch one of her old favourites.

When they reached home Lee would get to work. She turned back the duvet and puffed up the pillows on the 'big' bed in Janet's room. This is what Girls' Night is all about — Lee sitting up in bed next to Janet, with a tray filled with small bowls of party food on each of their laps.

'Are you ready, Mum?' Lee always checked as she reached for the remote.

One Saturday night some months later, as Lee was preparing to turn on the video machine, she waved the remote in the air and then put it down on the bed beside her.

'Now what? I'm ready and waiting,' Janet mused, but Lee, as usual, could not be rushed. She wriggled closer to Janet.

'You know that I'm not a child anymore. I'm an adult.'

'Yes. So?'

'We have to call this Women's Night.'

Before Lee could press the start button, Janet burst out laughing. Lee, not sure why she was laughing, joined her. When they had finally laughed themselves out, Lee aimed the remote and Women's Night was underway.

A week later Lee asked Janet if she had any ideas about which video they could hire. Janet shook her head. Lee screwed up her face and waited.

'So, Lee, what shall we do tonight?'

'Girls' Night, I mean Women's Night,' was the immediate reply.

'I know, but I thought we might need to do something different.'

'Why? Like what?'

Janet held up her hand, and pointing to one finger at a time she listed the possibilities.

'One, we could go for coffee. Two, we could go for a walk along the beach front. Three, we could watch TV. Four, we could sit together on the settee and have a chat. And five, we could just do nothing.'

'And?' Lee waited.

'And that's it.'

'No it's not, try and see what's on the other hand.'

Lee now has a girlfriend, Alison, who is the same age and who visits her once a week. She is a delightful young girl and a volunteer 'buddy'. Lee, unaware of Alison's volunteer status, looks forward to the visits and usually prepares a tray of her favourite snacks for their tea.

'It's a girls' kind of tea.'

'What exactly is that, Lee?'

With an exaggerated show of patience at my obvious ignorance, she explained slowly to me that it includes all the right 'stuff'.

'Like?'

'Like I make popcorn in the machine.'

'And? Is that what all the fuss is about?'

'I'm busy, Gran.'

Watching her moving deftly around the kitchen as she organised the nibbles, I was intrigued by her focussed concentration. Nothing was going to interrupt her. Scrupulously she measured out exactly the same amount of drink and food for each of them, and positively resisted any advice or assistance that Janet had the temerity to offer her.

'I know what I'm doing, Mummy.'

And this certainly appeared to be the case.

The two young girls eventually settle themselves in Lee's bedroom to watch either a video or a TV programme, during which they may also simultaneously play a fast card game of 'Snap', which causes shrieks of laughter. Alison explained that they can't play anything more complicated than this, as Lee either does not want to or considers it unnecessary to follow the rules. She is quite partial to making her own rules, which she considers to be more than sufficient. If it is a really hot day Alison drives her down to the beachfront for a cold drink and a walk, to see a movie, or they may just stroll around the mall looking at the clothes shops.

Lee enjoys the freedom of going off somewhere with a 'friend' and without Janet. This is a huge advance for someone who until now could not bear to have her mother out of her sight. Her association with Alison has both enhanced her self-confidence and quelled her anxiety about not having any friends. She appears to equate her time out with Alison as being the 'normal' life she so keenly wants to live.

During an interview with Alison she explained that she understands why it is difficult for Lee to befriend a girl of her own age.

'Our communication is similar to what a friendship between two girls of fourteen and nineteen would be. I can see that it would be difficult for her to be treated as an equal among her peers, which is a shame, as she would make a warm and giving friend.'

Alison elaborated further, citing some of Lee's current attitudes, like those towards boys, sex and her repeated verbal indignation about not being a child any more.

'Her attitudes are more like those of quite a young teenager.'

When asked what they talk about, she laughed.

'About the things she likes to do, listening to music, dancing and the usual things that young teenagers worry about.'

'Like?'

'Boys, Danny and John Stamos. She asks lots of questions about my boyfriends. She also complains about how her brothers constantly ask her to turn down her music, and about how her mother embarrasses her.'

'Sounds quite typical to me.'

'It is, but not for someone of eighteen. She quite delightfully told me about Danny's and her first kiss. She sometimes compares Danny and John Stamos. She has mentioned that Danny is also Down's. She's much more open and confident since she's had a relationship with Danny, and really likes to talk about it.'

'Has she told you that she's not a child?'

'Not exactly, but I know that my friends and I used to say that frequently when we were about fourteen. I think it's probably quite common at that age. Lee thinks a lot. I'm sure she understands much more than she can say, but sometimes I don't know what she's talking about. By the way, she doesn't stutter much when we chat.'

'Can you speak to her about anything deeper?'

'Yes, we sometimes discuss dying which she brought up one day. She was explaining that she once had a sister, but that she had died after only a few days of living.'

'That happened a long time before she was born.'

'Really! She gives the impression that she lost someone she knew and loved, although she did say that she was upset about not having had a chance to say goodbye to her. I think that when she's by herself she thinks a lot.'

'About what?'

'I'm not sure, but the way she comes out with things shows she's been thinking about them. She also tells me about her cousins in Australia.'

'What about them?'

'Oh, that she has long conversations with them on the phone. She tells them all about her Danny and John Stamos, and quite a lot of other stuff. They are two girls?'

'Yes, one is sixteen and the other is about to turn nineteen. They are wonderfully patient and manage to chat about all sorts of stuff, and they also laugh a lot during their conversations. Between the two of them they have managed to see her through her lack of close friends. She's been able to confide in them. What does she say about school?'

'She relates the facts of various events that happen during a day there, but she's quite unemotional about it and also doesn't seem to be very involved in it. One thing, before I forget. Lee is quite astonishing at the way she handles and plays on her keyboard thing. She's fast on the controls and sets it up for what she wants to play with ease and confidence. It's really quite complicated to set up. I do play the piano, so we frequently play on her keyboard together.'

'Is it hard spending time with her?'

'Not at all, we have a lot of fun together. I also spend 'care time' with two other Down's girls. One is six and the other is twelve, and the thing that is so interesting is that all three of them are quite different. Before I started doing this I had always simply boxed them as Down's and left it at that. So I'm enjoying finding out more about each of them as people, especially about Lee who is older and closer to my age group than they are. I think that I'm still in for some surprises from them all because of their individual differences.'

To feel the vulnerability of her existence, it seems necessary that Lee's story should follow the same fragmentary nature of her life as she reveals her feelings, ideas and opinions at unexpected moments. For her, continuity means having a regular general daily routine.

During the cold winter months of the school term she finds it almost impossible to get up and get ready for school. She wakes up early, but when Janet goes into her room to check on her progress she is not surprised to find Lee swaddled in her duvet with her earphones on and her journal on her lap. She is multi-tasking, listening, singing and writing furiously in her journal.

'Lee, you should be dressed by now.'

'I know.' She remains preoccupied.

'Lee, put that stuff away and get up… now!' Janet begins to apply some pressure.

Still no movement from Lee, who remains sitting in bed like a small pyjama-clad version of the Rock of Gibraltar.

'You're going to be late.'

'I know.'

Closing her book and removing her headphones, she looks appealingly into Janet's face.

'Must I?'

'You know you must.'

Lee shrugs. 'I tried.' She laughs and gets out of bed.

Time, as a directive, is not a part of her life. She is incapable of being hurried.

Having eventually made her way into the kitchen, she stands at the open door of the refrigerator and deliberates on its contents. Her choices are not made for the conventional eater of breakfasts, one of her more 'imaginative' breakfast concoctions being a mixture of cold rice, peas and tomato sauce on a toasted bagel. All this choosing and preparing uses up a considerable amount of time. Although Janet is becoming increasingly impatient, she is careful to hide this, as she knows that too much pressure on Lee at this point will only delay them further.

'Come on Lee – move it.'

'I'm moving it,' she calls back to Janet, as she carefully collects all of the items she needs to take to school. Swimming gear, Walkman, cell phone, notebooks and, of course, a snack for the mid-day break. She seldom forgets anything she may need at home. It remains for Janet to assess the weight and choice of clothing she has packed into her schoolbag. She is inclined to pack something that she fancies wearing, rather than something that might suit the weather of the day.

By the time they drive out of the gateway Janet has acquired another grey hair. Getting Lee ready to go anywhere is like a slow, laborious, major production with one exception – if she's going out with Danny.

Lee has a written school timetable, which she knows and follows closely. She likes to know in advance what is to happen each day. She has recently stopped asking about lunch as soon as she gets into the car. Food has become less of an event than it was before she became interested in Danny. She spends the rest of the school day afternoon in her bedroom with the door shut, and only emerges to get a drink from the kitchen or to go over some homework with Janet. Lee is happiest living within the routine that she knows and expects to be there.

'What do you do in your bedroom with the door shut, Lee?'

'Why do you want to know?'

'No good reason.'

'Well?'

'Well, what do you do there?'

'My life.'

I had my answer.

Could her day or anyone else's day have been explained more succinctly?

I stop to think about that life, where it's been and where it may be going. A young girl of eighteen often has her life-dream in front of her, a career to be chosen, marriage, motherhood and the years beyond. For Lee, life would probably follow a different road. She will stay at school for as long as it will be able to provide her with a stimulating learning situation. However, she would have to leave school when she turns twenty-one in three years' time. As yet no 'career' path has revealed itself.

Janet has encouraged Lee to help with her monthly market stall where she sells the gift items Lee has made at school. The school has enthusiastically helped Lee in this respect by setting up related projects to encourage her and foster her interest. They have shown her how to paint and decorate small boxes and to make pressed flower bookmarks, which she has done delicately and artistically. They have all sold extremely well. She is pleased with the sales, but has no concept of the value of the money she makes. It goes into her purse, where it may get forgotten or lost.

This deficiency in her commercial knowledge is partly due to her lack of comprehension of basic arithmetic. So far, she has been unable to grasp and relate to even the vaguest abstract meaning of addition and subtraction. This deficiency has not deterred Lee from trying to sort out the money and give the change to her customers. She is slow working out the money, but the customers are helpful and patient so Lee does not become flustered, and when she is too slow she graciously accepts a little help from Janet. She loves bagging and wrapping the parcels, which she invariably hands over to the customers with a shy 'don't-look-at-me' smile. Her most valuable contribution to the morning is the help she gives with the unpacking and positioning of the goods on the table. Although she is extremely careful as she performs all these duties, she is a long way from becoming a reliable shop assistant.

Her school work experience in the local supermarket where she tidied and packed shelves is unlikely to keep her interest long enough for it to become a full-time job. A part-time position is a possibility. The time she spends at the playschool making play dough is also a temporary job while she attends the school to which it belongs. Her teacher says that they are trying to encourage her to teach the children rather than to cuddle them.

At the moment she has no actual directional focus that could lead her into a career, a job and a way of earning money. Perhaps something will come up during the next two years. If not, she may go on to a vocational college. Life for Lee continues to be something of a serendipity experience.

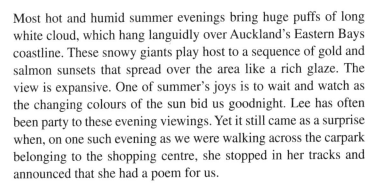

Most hot and humid summer evenings bring huge puffs of long white cloud, which hang languidly over Auckland's Eastern Bays coastline. These snowy giants play host to a sequence of gold and salmon sunsets that spread over the area like a rich glaze. The view is expansive. One of summer's joys is to wait and watch as the changing colours of the sun bid us goodnight. Lee has often been party to these evening viewings. Yet it still came as a surprise when, on one such evening as we were walking across the carpark belonging to the shopping centre, she stopped in her tracks and announced that she had a poem for us.

'Where is the poem, Lee?' Janet asked.

'Wait and I'll tell you.'

And this is what she recited.

'Stars and a cloud

The clouds are really light

And the stars are beautiful

And he made the world

A lovely place.'

Her face reflected the soft pink beauty of the early sunset as she spoke. A slight breeze lifted the dark hair that framed her face, adding an aching tenderness to the moment.

'Where did you get that poem from, Lee?' Janet asked.

'Oh Mummy, I made it up. Did you like it, Gran?'

'I certainly did. I didn't know you knew about poetry, Lee.'

'Well, Gran, you don't know everything.'

'That's true, but where did you learn about poetry?'

'We do it at school.'

'Have you made up any others, Lee?'

'Yes, one more.'

She was on a roll, so we stopped beside the car and waited for her to go on. Any interruption now might disperse her thought forever.

'It's about my music. Are you ready?' And without waiting for a reply she continued.

'I hear my song

And I can hear it

And it made the man in love

And it touches my heart.'

Another shortcoming in my understanding, I had not considered that Lee would understand or grasp the concept of poetry. That she might listen to a reading or try to read a poem herself was feasible, but that she should so ably compose her own was much further from my thinking.

This is one more lesson I have learnt— do not underestimate the ability of any person with Down syndrome to grasp concepts that they have not verbalised. Let their exposure to as much education as is possible set its own level. Lee has not offered any poetry since that day. It seems that she has moved on.

Moving on for Lee has been a major next step. She has fallen passionately and completely in love. But this time she is in love with a hometown boy who, quite delightfully, is in love with her. Although he is nine years older than she is, he also has Down syndrome, which has somewhat levelled the score. The young man in her life is her prom partner, Danny. Lee had said little about the dance except that, 'It was okay'. But it certainly must have been more than that, as it was the catalyst that changed their casual friendship into a relationship.

Danny is the caring attentive friend Lee has wanted all of her life. Their relationship started to gather pace with an exchange of e-mails, which were soon replaced by phone calls. Long teenage calls made and taken behind closed doors. Anyone entering Lee's bedroom while they were talking to each other was unceremoniously shushed out of the door by a waving, pointing hand. Soon a notice appeared on her bedroom door: 'Please do not enter when I talking to Danny'. This was followed by another: 'This is my room and I have my privacy'. Whispered declarations of love amidst giggles and sighs embellish their conversations as they explore their new-found feelings for each other.

'Where are we going?' has replaced her interest in the lunch menu as she gets into the car when Janet picks her up at the school gate. She is afraid that Janet may want to go shopping on the way home and so delay her phone access to Danny. She simply wants to get there as fast as possible, rush into her room, dump her school bag onto the floor and reach for the phone. Janet is attempting to teach her some restraint by making her wait so that Danny can call her.

'Lee, give Danny a chance. He may want to call you.'

'Why?'

'He might feel that he's doing something nice for you by being the one who does the phoning.'

'I can't wait for him. He's too slow.'

'It only seems too slow because you are too impatient. Anyway, it only seems fair to give him a chance too.'

Lee, unable to see the value in waiting, concedes to a sense of justice, and accepts Janet's explanation that Danny also needs a chance to call her. Filled with anticipation she moodily retires to her room to 'do her stuff', but rushes out every time the phone rings, hoping it will to be for her.

When Lee, all aglow, had announced that she was in love there was no doubt about what she had meant. Being in love for her has been a natural and unquestioning state. She is absolutely certain how she feels, but she is unable to explain even in the simplest terms how it makes her feel.

'Lee, how do you actually feel when you say that you're in love?'

'Fine.'

'Is that it, just fine? It's got to be better than that.' Silence. 'Do you feel like singing and smiling all the time?'

'Maybe, Gran.' Lee gave this some thought and she seemed to be struggling with the idea. Then quite suddenly her mood changed, she became annoyed and told me off.

'Why do you ask me, Gran, when I already told you?' She flashed her eyes at me. 'There is such a thing as privacy.'

Lee so seldom shows any anger. Perhaps being in love has helped her to release her feelings more than she has been able to do so far. It was time for me to back off.

Their relationship is as tempestuous as it is beautiful. Neither of them is able to allow the other to form or enjoy any other friendship. Even a same-sex casual and meaningless chat becomes a cause for rising emotions and tears. Lee is jealous of Danny's workmates, and he becomes infuriated with her if she speaks to any boy during their ten pin bowling sessions at their club. He is particularly keen that she should give up on John Stamos, a matter she has agonised over, but decided to continue. She wisely no longer mentions his name to Danny.

Unfortunately, it is impossible to help her to unravel and understand these emotions, mainly because she is unable to grasp the idea that relationships can weather a few storms without becoming annihilated. It is heartbreaking to see how easily she can become stranded and devastated as she tries to cope with these fluctuating emotions. She simply does not have the ability to reach out for explanations or reasons that could help keep her afloat when she needs reassurance.

She vehemently rejects any help or comfort from all of us, leaving her no option but to tread water within the concentric circles of the limitations that make up her life. Tear-stained and dejected, once again she retires to her bedroom and eventually drowns herself in music.

———◆◆◆◆◆———

There are times when Lee enjoys being teased about Danny. She replies with giggles and weak protests.

'Lee, is Danny your boyfriend?'

'What do you think?'

'Well the last time I asked you if Danny was your boyfriend you told me I was crazy.'

'Yes, but now is another time.'

'I take that as being a "yes"?'

'If you like.'

'Come on, Lee, are you his girlfriend or not?'

'I suppose so.'

'That's better. Are you pleased about that?'

'Of course.'

Lee had suddenly come a long way from 'maybe'.

'Has he told you that he loves you?'

'Gran!'

'Well?'

Lee lowered her voice and blushed.

'Yes, he did.'

'And what did you say?'

'I told him it's okay.'

'Did you tell him that you love him too?'

'Of course.' Then with a look of disdain she added, 'What do you think?'

'I think it sounds good.'

Having established the basics, we are now able to have frequent conversations about the subject. Lee has assembled a collage photograph of the two of them, which she placed in a purple frame. It has been given pride of place on her bedside table.

This smiling reminder of their relationship goes everywhere with her. It even accompanies her to my house when she sleeps over. She carefully and lovingly sets it up on my bedside table. However, her interest in John Stamos remains as strong as ever.

Turning eighteen and almost simultaneously falling in love has initiated an enormous change in Lee. She has begun to assert herself, to make her presence felt, at least now and again. She is able to concede some changes in her daily routine with more agility and acceptance than she might have done previously.

When Alison needed to give more time to her own studies she stopped coming to visit Lee. She accepted the break, the reasons for it, and the introduction of a new replacement friend with surprising ease. Shortly after this, her long-time teacher aid, Kathy, had to give up teaching. Janet, concerned about the upheaval this might create for Lee at school, was clearly worried about how she would take this news. Would Lee decide not to go to school if Kathy was not there? How much did Lee rely on Kathy for support? Could she sustain her progress without her? Would all the care and build-up Lee had been receiving at school be erased at this late stage? Should her approach to Lee be with spin, or reason and logic?

This predicament reminded us of one we had faced many years ago when Janet's young four-year-old brother suddenly refused to go to nursery school. At first he would not get out of the car at the school gates, and then he threw a tantrum in the house before getting to the front door. Having spoken to his teacher, we were reasonably sure there was nothing in particular that threatened him there. Unless, of course, it was the teacher herself that he was rebelling against.

We decided to let him stay home for a few days, hoping his attitude might change. But on the Monday morning of his going back he started his objections all over again. Frustrated, I yelled at him.

'All right, all right, then stay home and waste all of Daddy's money. He has already paid for this term.'

He stopped performing and stood still, looking at me.

'Why didn't you tell me that before?' he asked with seemingly genuine interest. He picked up his bag and walked to the door.

The last reason I would have thought of giving to a four-year-old child was an economic one. We never had cause to discuss it again. The lesson we learnt from this was that reason and logic might be understood by the most unlikely-seeming recipients, and in the most unlikely situations.

Relying on this past success, Janet explained to Lee that Kathy had some reasons of her own why it would be difficult for her to continue in her job of teaching. Lee listened intently, and then asked what the reasons were. She was satisfied with the explanation Janet gave to her and eased into her new school situation without a ripple of trauma.

She now phones Kathy and chats for ages about Danny, about school, and naturally with complaints about various members of the family who may have annoyed her. She simply redeployed Kathy from teacher to friend. Little did Janet think that Lee's entrée into logic would return to confound her. One evening, on their way to the parking garage after seeing a mildly romantic movie, Lee started mumbling something to Janet about Danny.

'Speak up, Lee, I don't know what you're talking about.'

Lee became frustrated and began to stutter badly.

'It doesn't matter,' she finally managed to say.

'Maybe it does matter, Lee. If you've something to say, please say it. I'm listening.'

'I told you, it's nothing.' Then it all flooded out. 'I told you that Danny is my boyfriend and I want to know why I can't sleep with him. You are sleeping with Dad.'

This was not the first time that Lee had broached this subject, but it became the first time that she would not give up until she got the answer that she wanted.

'I told you, Lee, you have to be married like Dad and I are. Then you can do what you like.'

The sex education Lee had received at school, added to what she may have picked up from other sources, left Janet in some doubt as to the depth of what Lee was asking. It was possible that she may have just wanted to sleep in a bed with Danny.

'I'm not saying that I want to get married. I'm saying why can't I sleep with Danny?'

'It's like I said. You can when you are married.'

'Well my brothers aren't married and they sleep with their girlfriends.' Lee's reply had an edge of annoyed defiance. Janet noted this and counted it as another milestone in her maturing personality. Unable to refute this unmistakable chunk of logic, Janet gave up.

'Then I suppose you can too, but perhaps you'll need to talk it over with Danny first.'

'I know that… and even whatever you say, I'm going to do it.'

Having successfully got her point made, the rebel connected herself to her Walkman and the matter was dropped.

Later I asked Janet what she thought Lee would do next.

'I don't know for sure. Probably nothing. She's brought this up a couple of times before, though not with so much conviction. We'll just have to wait and see how it goes.'

A word with Danny, if he was willing, now seemed appropriate.

'Danny, you know that we are doing a book about Lee's life, and now that you two have got together I wondered if you would like to say a few words about yourself.'

'How do you mean?'

'Well, for example, Lee has spoken about all sorts of things for this book including a bit about you. I hope you don't mind?'

Danny looked at Lee, who smiled her confirmation back at him from the edge of her bed on which we were all sitting. Reassured, he nodded his approval.

'That's okay, what do you want to know?'

'We'll do it like a TV interview. I'll ask you some questions and you can also ask me some if you want to. Also, if you don't like the questions you don't have to answer them. Is that all right?'

'Yes,' Danny replied quickly, He was interested and wanted to get on with it.

'Good. We can start with a chat about girlfriends. Have you had a girlfriend before — before Lee that is?'

'I hadn't really thought about it before, but I hoped to have one some day so that we could hang out together.' Danny, clearly sensitive to Lee's feelings, glanced quickly at her. But Lee, who was looking at me, missed this contact. Danny read this as being a signal that he was not embarrassing her and felt more confident about proceeding.

'Do you get a lot of phone calls from friends?'

'Not really. I had this friend and we used to phone a lot, but it is not so much now. I enjoy talking to Lee.'

'That's good, what sort of things do you speak about?'

Without any hesitation Danny replied, 'The future.'

'What about the future, Danny, can you give me an example?'

'Me and her together, maybe. We'll have to see how it goes. I have to keep it all under control.'

'Do you mean living together?'

'Ya, one day.'

That will cost money.'

'That's all right. I have a bank account.'

'And you have a job.'

'Yes, but I'm hoping for a change so I can do something else. It's almost ten years that I'm doing the same job and I want something different career-wise. I can't be sorting letters forever. But work is very important to me.'

'In what way?'

'For paying bills, the electricity, like my father does. I want to do what my father has done for lots of years.'

'Do you want to be a father one day?'

'I hope I'd be a good father, teach manners, have ground rules and do jobs around the house like my father does.'

'Are you getting tired, Danny?'

'No, no let's go on.'

'What would you expect from your wife?'

'I would not make stress on her. I'd help her with the children and the housework and go shopping.'

'What would you do for fun?'

'Spend time with my wife and my children.' Danny put his arm around Lee who looked blissfully up into his face.

'If you didn't have any children would it be a big disappointment to you?'

'Not really, but I like children. One day I can show you a video about me.'

Like Lee, Danny enjoys watching videos relating to his own childhood.

'Do you know how sex works? Lee had talks about sex at school. Do you know how babies are made?'

'My sister-in-law had a son two years ago. Parents have children.'

Sensing that Danny was not quite comfortable with the directness of this line of questioning, we changed direction.

'Right Danny, what about gym? When you are married and a husband, will you still go to gym to keep your figure in shape?'

Both Lee and Danny burst out laughing. Lee playfully punched his biceps.

'Of course I will. I will have to look nice for my wife.'

Lee, who had not interrupted or said anything throughout this 'interview', nodded her approval.

'So this fit man would go to work, and then come home in the evening and have the dinner his wife had made for him, and then what?'

'This is a hard one.'

'Not really, you'd go to bed.' Danny nodded. 'And ?'

'I'd hold my wife in my arms.' Lee blushed. 'And I'd kiss her.' Lee beamed.

'And then would you make love? Have you a good idea how that works?'

'I would hope... I'd try to learn about it first. It's like driving a car, you can't just drive, you have to have lessons and learn about it before you can start the car.'

'Fair enough.'

'We would visit the grandparents and they'll give the children sweets.'

Danny has clearly given his future some thought and appears to have shaped a sequence of events, modelled largely on his family's life, which he hopes will eventuate. He wants to be the father and husband that he sees his father to be.

At twenty-eight, Danny is a delightful, sensitive and honest young man. He is significantly more confident than Lee is and just as open. As I gathered my notes from the bed, they linked arms and left the room. They were ready for their night out together.

Not wanting to ask Danny what he thought of having Down syndrome in case it would be disturbing for him as a subject, a call to his mother seemed a good idea.

'Linda, I just wanted to tell you that 'interviewing' Danny was most enjoyable, enlightening and rewarding.'

'That's good, was he cooperative?

'Extremely. There was one point that I wanted to bring up, but as I hadn't cleared it with you I thought that I had better do so first. It's about how Danny feels about having Down syndrome.'

'Oh, that's all been discussed some time ago. When he first realised he was different from his brothers and other boys, we explained that he had Down syndrome and how this had come about.'

'Did he understand it all?'

'Absolutely. He knows that it is a chromosome aberration and he accepts that it cannot be changed.'

'Is he miserable about this? Lee hates having Down's.'

'He doesn't talk about it anymore, but he did say at the time that it was a great pity that he had Down's because he would have liked to have been able to have gone for a beer at the pub with friends like the other boys do. Of course, he didn't really have any friends either.'

'Has having a girlfriend for the first time had any obvious affect on him?'

'Definitely, he's on top of the world.'

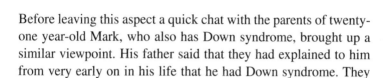

Before leaving this aspect a quick chat with the parents of twenty-one year-old Mark, who also has Down syndrome, brought up a similar viewpoint. His father said that they had explained to him from very early on in his life that he had Down syndrome. They also told him how it had come about, and that there was nothing they could do about it, but that they all loved him anyway.

As he got older he did comment that he really did not like having Down's, but if there was absolutely nothing that they could do about it he would just have to get on with life. To his credit he has done just that. After finishing his schooling, he attended classes at a technical college and is now working for one of the big supermarket chains. He is a happy young man with a ready smile and a devoted girlfriend.

This, her eighteenth year, has also given Lee the facility to expand into a number of new activities. She is reading quite well and is content to spend a lot of time in a bookshop or at the library looking through books that interest her. She is extremely comfortable on the computer, and surfs the net studiously bookmarking her choices without any help. She enjoys working on the computer and types at ever-increasing speeds, spending many hours checking the various sites to do with her beloved John Stamos, whose photographs she avidly prints out. Most of all she now has friends to do 'girls' stuff' with.

Shelly, who took over when Alison left, is full of fun and a great success. And Lee has Danny to love. She has also become a committed telephone call-maker. Receiving phone calls is a major delight for her, especially as she previously saw this as something that only happened to other people. She feels part of 'the scene', and happily calls her cousins in Australia to discuss in great detail what is currently happening between Danny and her. Her life and her sense of self have expanded.

It is still not possible to have an in-depth conversation of any length with Lee. Her insights, which do not appear to be triggered by anything specific, burst through spontaneously at odd times. She has developed a strong sense of privacy and of personal space. Her conceptual ability has strengthened, but there is no telling at this stage exactly how far this can go. At the moment it is a question of being grateful for every step forward, however small or slow it may be.

If it were possible to characterise life with Lee, it would be that between her fondness and adherence to routine she is unpredictable. She has and does provide us all with so much fun and laughter, with her quirky sense of humour and her open approach to most things that we may generally regard as off-beat. She could never be considered as having been a naughty child and, even now, as a supposedly rebellious teenager, she is headstrong and obstinate rather than disobedient. Her unpredictability can be considered to be initiative. Take for instance her 'brush with the law'.

Lee is afraid of rainstorms, especially when they are accompanied by thunder. Janet, well aware of her fear, usually appeared at her bedside the moment a storm broke. But one night when Janet was away in Sydney for a short break, Lee's fear was put to the test.

A huge thunderous storm engulfed the city at about 2am, waking Lee but not David or any of her brothers, who were all sound asleep in the house. Not seeing Janet at her bedside, and forgetting that her mother was away, she called out for her. Not getting an answer, she called again but the noise of the storm drowned her voice. She panicked as the family slept on.

Suddenly, David was woken by a loud knocking on the front door. He tumbled out of bed, and half-asleep he opened the door to find two policemen standing there.

'Is this the Jackson house?'

'Yes?' he mumbled.

'Are you David Jackson?' David's sleepy lack of conviction aroused his suspicion.

'Yes, what's wrong?' A sudden thought that one of his sons may have had an accident and was not at home and in bed, as he believed to be the case, sent a cold chill through him. He was now wide awake.

'Do you live here, sir?'

'Yes, is there something wrong?'

'We've had a rather distressing call from a young girl, Lee.'

'What! Sorry, what did you say?'

The officer repeated his statement, and then asked if she was there.

'Yes, she's here, she's asleep.'

'Can we see her, sir?'

David led the two policemen into Lee's bedroom where they found her in bed and fast asleep.

'Why are you looking for her?' David needed to make some sense of this all.

'During the height of the storm we got a 111 call from a young girl who gave her name as Lee and, according to our information, she was extremely distressed.'

Finally it was all sorted out. Lee, not having Janet on hand, and not being able to wake David, decided that 111 was the next best move. But by the time the police arrived, the rain had stopped and she had gone back to sleep.

Notwithstanding how strange the night had been for David, he and everyone else was delighted that Lee had shown that she had the presence of mind to phone 111 when she felt cornered. What one could not know was if she would ever do it again if she needed help.

Lee's sense of right and wrong has a number of limitations as well as a leaky edge. She is aware of basic social behavioural requirements and is careful not to transgress these. Her judgement is less reliable when it comes to doing something that she has set her heart on doing. This was particularly evident when she was younger.

For some time Lee, then aged eight, had asked to be allowed to drive the car. Janet's explanations that she had to be a 'grown-up' and have a licence did not satisfy her, and she constantly asked about driving.

One afternoon, when Janet and David were visiting a friend who had recently bought a new van, Lee took matters into her own hands. We had all seen and admired the van before we went into the house. Later, when Janet called Lee to come in for tea and got no answer, she went out onto the deck to see where she was. As she looked across the lawn she saw that the van was rolling backwards down the drive. We all ran outside, but were not in time to stop it from backing into the garden wall. Sitting in the driver's seat was a small and perplexed little girl.

'I told you I can drive,' she piped up, not realising what she had done.

Our friend's husband was wonderful. He carefully removed Lee from the van, checked to see that she was not hurt, and then explained that it was not a good idea for her to drive without a licence. He then made her promise not to do it again. They had a cuddle and we all went back into the house to finish our tea. Our offer to pay for the damage was refused.

That she had proved her point seemed to have satisfied Lee, as she did not try to drive again. However she did not really understand that what she had done was wrong. Her sense of consequence is still unreliable.

It is Lee's good fortune to have been born at a time, and perhaps into a culture, that has been able to provide her with the possibility of a structured, stable and protected life. She has been further blessed by belonging to a family which has a strong and resilient structure and which has accepted and fully integrated her into the unit.

Now towards the end of her eighteenth year, she sees herself as part of the adult family and wastes no time in correcting anyone who may attempt to patronise her. She has half-abandoned her box of toys, and rarely plays with or shows any interest in them, and does not object when Janet selects items to be given away to a charity. However, she still likes to sleep with her big old soft furry monkey beside her.

Although her move out of childhood has been slow, it is now almost over. It has left behind it a very young adult who is still carrying a number of unresolved teenage problems, but who has retained the freshness and innocence of her childhood. One of the issues she still has to grapple with is the extremely uneven relationship between her emotional and intellectual development. Perhaps time will help resolve it for her.

PART THREE

FAMILY

What of Lee's brothers? What has it been like for them growing up with Lee in the centre and on the edge of their lives? During our separate discussions, these three young men gave freely and honestly as they drew deeply from their innermost thoughts and emotions.

Settling himself stiffly on the settee opposite me, Andy, who is just less than three years younger than Lee, is the only one who has not known what life was like without her. Consequently, he is the one who could have been most affected by her presence.

I watched and waited as this blonde, fresh-faced youth settled into the corner of the settee, letting his legs sprawl boyishly out in front of him. The grandmother in me mused lovingly as I watched my young grandson narrow his sky-blue eyes and assemble his thoughts in preparation for our discussion. At the same time, I saw a serious young man who is still in the throes of organising and managing his own teenage problems. In this respect he might be closer to understanding Lee than his brothers.

'Andy, before we get started I want you to know that if there is anything you feel you would rather not answer, I will understand and respect that.'

'Oh no, it's okay, I'm okay.'

'Good. It's just that I'd rather have no answer than one you may think I want to hear.'

'Gran, I understand.'

It was more likely that it was I who had some trepidation about hearing what he or his brothers might come up with during these discussions. For all of us, this was an area which we had not explored in any depth. I gave them each the same option of not discussing any areas that they felt was off-limits for them. They all agreed to be as frank as they could.

Andy, usually keen to get away, was waiting for me with an unusual display of patience.

'Andy, do you remember when it was that you realised that your sister was different and how you felt about it?'

'I think I realised it when I was about six or seven. It didn't bother me, I just accepted it.'

'Has it been difficult growing up with her?'

He gazed into the distance, as if trying to retrieve and relive some of his past. So much is crowded into ten years of a young teenager's life that it could be more difficult for him to recall his memories than it is for someone much older. Shaking his head as he looked back at me, he answered slowly.

'It's just been normal for me. I haven't, and don't know, any different really. She's just a part of the family. Maybe not as fast as everyone else, but then we're all different anyway.'

'What, if anything, does she contribute to the general family life, to your life?'

He smiled and cocked his head to one side.

'She has a really good sense of humour, and she sometimes jokes with me. That is, when she gives me the time of day.' I laughed. He became serious again. 'I think she likes to be private – maybe she feels that she can't express herself around other people, but can in her music and TV.'

The sun began to filter through the net curtain behind him. Its light sparkled over his number one haircut, turning each hair into a fibre optic thread. He was now relaxed and enjoying looking into areas that he had previously not given much thought to. He was ready, and I sensed that any delay might disrupt and change his easy manner.

'Andy, how often do you manage to chat with her?'

'Not too often, just sometimes, and then it could be about nothing much. It could be about what she's doing or has done.'

'I realise that you are in different years at school, but do you ever bump into her there and, if so, does she acknowledge you?'

'We don't see each other too often, but when she does see me she usually waves to me or says hello. If we really bump each other, or are very close by, she doesn't stop to talk but just gives me a pat and goes on her way.'

'What sort of comments do your friends make?'

'Well they don't really know her or how to act – I think they're scared of the idea of someone with a problem.'

'This may be an unfair or difficult question, Andy, but how do you think she'll make out in the future? It's just your opinion I'm asking for.'

Andy took his time over this one.

'She's a positive person. She's aware of being different and it must be annoying. Perhaps it's because people look at her. She may not understand it all, but she's certainly aware. It's not going to be easy.'

'What sort of effect do you think she's had on the family in general?'

During our conversation I discovered a depth of understanding that this quiet sixteen-year-old boy mostly keeps hidden beneath his daily teenage life. And I was quite overwhelmed by his consummate summing up of the situation.

'We have all learnt something positive from having her around, but it's not worth it for her to have had a spoilt life for us to be able to learn this.'

Jason, who is approaching his twenty-first birthday, has a creative and witty facade which belies the analytical and creative breadth of his thinking. He has a delightfully playful relationship with Lee, and has always had a great capacity to amuse her. We sat side-by-side on an old couch under a window at the end of the kitchen.

It was the last Sunday morning of the university holidays, and probably my last chance of having his undivided attention for any length of time. I smiled to myself as I watched his long lanky frame ease itself into a comfortable position. His energy and vitality sang out to me.

'So Ma, where do we start?'

'I suppose a good place would be if you could remember back to when it was that you first realised that Lee had a problem. I know you were very young when she was born, so I expect it took a while.'

Jason nodded as his thoughts came racing in.

'Well Ma, it was not an isolated moment, it was a progressive thing for me. I never felt that she was Down's, but just that she was Lee. I've never seen her as a Down's girl. I've just taken her for who she is… actually I couldn't imagine her any other way. But of course, I know that she is different.'

'So how has her being in the family affected you personally?'

'Only in the way that it must have made me more open-minded towards handicapped people, perhaps more sensitive to their needs. And yet that's funny, as I haven't really seen her as a handicapped person.'

'I know what you mean. When we're having fun or doing something together she's just one of the family. She only stands out when she is slow or stuck on something she can't grasp. Do you manage to talk to each other easily — you know, just talk about stuff?'

'All the time. We talk about everything… and nothing.' A private smile fluttered across Jason's face as he recalled some of their encounters. 'Most of it was more humourous than serious. In a way it was almost like not talking, but more like word playing that becomes a chat. You couldn't call it a conversation.'

'Did you enjoy this?'

'Oh yes, I like to make her laugh. She doesn't laugh that easily, but I seem to know how to do it. She has a lovely laugh that is so natural.'

'You were still at school with her for a while when she started there. Did you have any contact with her during the day?'

'Yes, I did. I remember one occasion especially. I happened to be walking past her classroom, and as I looked in I saw that the teacher was giving her a hard time. The more she repeated the question the more upset and stubborn Lee became.'

'So what did you do about it?'

'I went in and explained to the teacher that I was her brother and that her approach would never work. To give her some credit she listened to me and gave Lee a break.'

Jason got up and filled the kettle. 'Tea?' I nodded waiting for him to go on.

'As you know, Ma, with Lee if things aren't going well the only way to get her right is to try a new tack before she shuts down and you get nowhere.'

'She must have been pleased to have you around for back-up.'

'I think so, although she never said anything about it afterwards. She must have felt safe having us there. She always waved to me when we saw each other.'

'What did your friends think or say about her? How did they react?'

'If they saw her around at school they always waved to her. Those friends of mine who have met her, or who have come to the house, relate to her easily. You remember Mark? When he came to the house he always made time to chat to her, and because of this she made an effort to come out of her room when he was here.'

'How do you think she'll make out in the future? What sort of a life do you think she has ahead of her?'

'Don't know, haven't thought about it. Anyway, you can't predict anyone's future.'

We had once discussed the seemingly shortened life span of an adult with Down syndrome, and he was visibly taken aback at the possibility of this event. It was clear that he was not going to go anywhere near this subject.

'Your friends notwithstanding, do you think boys in your age group can handle handicapped people?'

He handed me my tea, and shook his head as he let himself sink back onto the old couch.

'Generally speaking, they're pretty ignorant and are likely to make fun of them, use them in jest. It's just ignorance and a huge lack of understanding. And perhaps a lack of real exposure to them.'

'Jason, does Lee ever initiate a chat with you?'

'Of course, it works both ways.'

'I remember that you used to be the one that could best babysit her, the one that could get her to do whatever it was that she had to do. Perhaps that's still true. Why do you think that is?'

'Our babysitting was never hard work – she's my sister you know. Anyway she's easy. Mostly she entertains herself, and if I need to tell her to do something like get ready for bed, she listens easily if the instructions are made into a game.'

Jason was relaxed and enjoying the exploratory nature of our talk, and he was a spontaneous fountain of recollections and comments.

'Jase, you seem to imply that apart from being playful she has a good sense of humour. Am I right?'

'That she does. She loves it when I bump or hurt myself. If I cry out she enjoys a hearty laugh at my expense. I use this sometimes when she's in one of her down phases, and it usually works. She can be manipulated, but not always.'

'That's true. I'm sometimes unable to pull her out of a low period too, but isn't she wonderful when she's on a high? She's so full of life and energy and quips. I love it when she takes command and gives instructions that she doesn't really expect anyone to carry out.'

'I know. I'm not always successful either. She goes through such extreme feelings, big highs and big lows – by being silly I can usually get her out of them, but if she's too low I just leave her to get over it herself.'

Jason was alight with thoughts and anecdotes and I did not want to divert him.

'What other games do you play with her?'

'Well, they are a variety of unorthodox games, ones I've made up really. For example, if I say something to her and she answers, as she often does, "yes right", I say, "yes left". It becomes a game for who gets the last word.'

'You seem to have lots of quality and fun time with her.' I smiled as I imagined the two of them building up a crescendo of laughter as they topped each other's words.

'If you know the TV shows that she watches you can play with those too. She is full-on with quoting sayings she's picked up from them, and she has an endless supply.'

'Is there anything else that you wanted to say?'

We were both silent for a moment as Jason considered the question.

'Well it's a bit unrelated.'

'That's okay, carry on.'

'When she's really upset, say over something that's happened between her and Danny, and I mean upset enough to cry, she often turns to me to let it all out. I think that Mum and I are the two that relate best to her.'

'Why do you think that is?'

'I think that it's because we both have a creative looseness that she responds to.' Jason withdrew then said softly. 'I can't imagine what life would be like without her.'

'Jase, there is only one more thing I want to ask you.'

He suddenly seemed tired, but turned to me and nodded, waiting for the question.

'We can leave off now and carry on later if you like.' I could see that all that he had given had caused him to search deeper than he had realised.

'No, I'd rather we finish off now if you're okay.'

'Right. Well, what sort of impact do you think Lee's had on the family?'

'Huge – especially on our parents. She's given my mother a full-time job. She's given her an ongoing responsibility for maintaining and entertaining someone for the rest of her life. And on top of that she still has to look after everyone else.'

It was my turn to nod. I have seen my daughter spread herself paper-thin at times to cope with it all, but she manages it and has never complained.

'You know, Gran, it's even in the simple things like making sure that Lee has a comfortable body temperature because she doesn't seem to notice when she's too hot or too cold. Perhaps she hasn't got the usual body thermometers that should indicate her condition to her. Mum really has to watch her like a hawk.'

In some ways being the oldest in the family may have been an advantage for Jake, as he was old enough to accept an explanation from Janet that Lee was, and would always be, different from the rest of the family. He also accepted from Janet that Lee would require some help and patience from him, but he did not see this as an immediate problem because he had no real contact with her. She was 'just a baby' and he was busy being a little boy.

However, being a bright and serious five-year-old child, he was well aware of the replaced axis to which the family was now pinned. After a few months he carefully and gently questioned Janet and David about Lee's condition, trying not to upset them, but trying to understand what had happened so that he could sort it out for himself. These early seeds of consideration and sensitivity to the plight of people close to him have matured and become a significant part of his personality.

Jake is now an independent twenty-four year-old young man. Having finished his schooling by the age of sixteen, he took himself off to see the world and landed in Korea where he spent almost a year. He followed this up with an economics degree at university and is now a young businessman who works and 'plays' with great enthusiasm. We share the special pleasure of a strong mutual respect and empathy for each other.

'Jake, at what stage did you realise that Lee was different?'

'Right away, really. Mum told me when she came home from the hospital. I came out of the house into the driveway to meet them and she showed me the baby and told me. Actually she just looked like a baby. I don't think that I got the real meaning of it then.'

'How did you feel about it?'

'I felt sorry for Mummy, even though I wasn't quite sure of it all.'

'As time went by, did having Lee around bother you?'

'It only became a big deal when I had to tell my mates about it.'

Jake made a quick sideways nod. 'I got a lot of sympathy from them and a lot more from their parents.'

'Did that make you uncomfortable?'

'Not really.'

'Can you recall what the daily life of the family was like then?'

'It was a long time ago, Ma, and a lot has happened since then, so it's not so easy to remember.'

I thought that perhaps the return to this early childhood period may be painful for him and that perhaps I should move on. His cell phone rang.

'Hello, yes, okay I'll call you back.'

'Do you want to stop now, Jake?'

'No, Ma, they can wait.'

'Where were we?'

'I remember that Mum was always concerned about Lee, twice as concerned as seemed normal.'

'Could you play with her?'

'Not really. She liked to kiss a lot, then she wouldn't, then she'd give a heap of hugs, then she wouldn't give any. I remember that she was very strong and could push quite hard. She was much stronger than she looked.'

'Did you ever have to do anything for her or look after her?'

'She was shielded from most difficulties by the amount of effort that Mummy put in, or I would probably have had to do more.'

'What about now, what sort of contact do you have with her?'

'I try to chat with her but it's always quite strained – she wants to come and talk to me, but she often gets lost in the words and then gets quite frustrated.'

'How is she when you take her out to eat or to a movie? I see that she gets all dressed up to go with you.'

'She's fairly quiet, but I know that she loves the whole outing.'

'Has having a sister with Down's made a difference to your attitude to handicapped people?'

'I could say that it's made me more sensitive, but I don't know that it has. I don't really know how different I would have been towards them if it hadn't been for her. I do feel that I notice Down's people more than I may have done otherwise.' Jake paused, glancing at the cat who was sunning himself on the windowsill, then looked straight back at me, his dark brown eyes meeting mine. 'You know Mummy has the whole stress of it and has left us all fairly free.'

'Now at eighteen, how do you see Lee entering life as a young woman?'

'Well, she clearly wants more involvement in what's going on. She tries to participate. She likes to be with and talk to the girls (his and Jason's girlfriends). She really wants to join in.'

'How does she show this?'

'If we're sitting in the room she wanders in and says "Hi". She especially likes to touch and fiddle with their hair or give them a relaxing shoulder massage.'

'Do they mind?'

'Oh no, they're very friendly and let her get on with it. She gives a good massage.'

'Do you think she's happy?'

'It's hard to say, she lives in her own world and seems to get lost in it sometimes. She can entertain herself for such long periods, drawing and singing and dancing. I think she gets caught in a repetitive loop, or perhaps she is just short of a variety of tools to engage herself otherwise.'

'Jake, I think she appears to have more logic in her thinking these days. What do you think?'

'Yes, I agree. She can take an idea and develop it further, which she didn't seem to be able to manage before. I also think that having a boyfriend has made her feel more like us. It's given her some sort of acceptance in herself.'

'Is there anything that you want to add?'

Jake gave this some thought.

'Well it's rather strange, but when I was away in Korea I missed her a lot. I'm not sure why. Then one day she wrote me a really nice letter telling me how much she misses me and loves me. That was special.'

'Oh, one more thing, how do you think she sees her future?'

'Her ambitions are soap opera driven, probably not too unlike many other naive young girls.'

His cell phone rang again.

'Answer it darling, we're finished.'

'Thank you, Ma.'

Lee has three brothers who will always be there for her.

Sitting quietly at the computer, Lee appeared to be studying some text on the internet.

'Hi Lee. What are you reading?'

'Gran, I'm busy.'

'I can see that. I was just wondering what you found so interesting.'

'I want to find out about John Stamos's sister. I don't know what she does for work.'

'Never mind John Stamos, Lee, what about Danny? You are taking him to the school ball again aren't you?'

Lee made me wait while she bookmarked her place, and closed down the computer before giving my question any sort of recognition.

Still facing the computer, she gave a much more detailed answer than I expected.

'He put a hand on my leg and the other hand on my neck and asked me if I've been kissed.'

'When was this?'

'Before.'

'So what did you say?'

'Of course I want to be kissed. He must try to understand how much I feel. I don't want him to be cross.'

'How do you feel?'

'Well, Gran, I've never been in love before and I want someone I can trust.'

'What do you mean by trust?'

'Well, Jason said that I mustn't be jealous with Danny.'

Lee understood the concept and offered the best explanation she could.

'Jason gave you good advice.'

'I suppose. I don't know why, Gran, but my brothers call me names.'

'What on Earth do you mean?'

'Like I said, they call me funny names.'

'Such as?'

'I dunno, like babe, cookie, snooks – I don't like it.'

'They know that, Lee, they're teasing you. Those are loving names.'

'I don't think so.'

'Do you think a name is important?'

'Pa...leese! What do you think! Of course.'

Lee is reluctant to enter into a conversation or even a room if she thinks that the people in or around her do not know her name. She feels a strong identity with her name and does not feel at all comfortable or confident being separated from it. Her name is extremely important to her; it seems to tell her and reaffirm for her who she is.

'Gran?'

'Yes, Lee?'

'Jake said that I can't have sex with John Stamos.'

'Oh… What is sex, Lee?'

'Gran, I can't say that to you.'

'You just did.'

'No, I just told you what Jake said to me.'

'Well, what did you say back to him?'

'That's not what I'm talking about.'

'What are you talking about?'

'I'm talking about John Stamos and you don't understand.'

'I think I do. I think Jake wanted to explain that John Stamos is far away so sex or any other kind of meeting isn't really possible.'

'I know that. But I can go to America to see him, maybe at his house.'

'What about his wife, Rebecca? Is that her name?'

'I don't want to talk about them.'

Ignoring me, Lee turned on the computer, and so far as she was concerned that was that.

———◆◆✕◆◆———

Lee has now been to her second school ball with Danny, and once again she has returned home glowing with the pleasure of it all. It seemed that it might be interesting to find out from Lee how the two dances compared with each other, and how Danny felt about it. Janet's inquiry had not met with any success. Lee simply shut off any discussion by telling her that, 'It was okay', and that she did not need to ask any more questions.

'Lee, do you know that Gran is still writing a book about you?'

'I do. What about my brothers?'

'No, she thinks that you're more interesting.'

'Does she know I'm Down's?'

'Of course, I told her long ago. How do you know that you're Down's?'

'Hello there, it's me,' she laughed.

Her elevated mood gave me the idea that this may be a good time to discuss the dance.

'Lee, you haven't told me anything about this school ball that you and Danny went to.' And by way of reinforcement I added that it might need to be included in our book. Lee was not impressed, and instead got up and went into her room and shut the door. This was one subject that Lee was not going to discuss.

However, because Danny and Lee had been picked up and brought back from the ball by one of Lee's teachers, and had not been taken by Janet as before, we were particularly interested in how she had handled the whole event.

About ten minutes later I was sitting watching TV when Lee appeared in the doorway.

'Do you want to watch this programme, Lee?'

She did not answer, but thrust a small scrap of paper under my nose. As I tried to figure out exactly what she had in mind, she dropped it onto my lap and went back to her room. I picked the paper up and read the following hastily scrawled note:

'Gran, on Friday a woman came to get me and my boyfriend, we dance and we dance together quite slowly. We kiss and we dance.'

Lee had finished with chats, discussions and interviews. I was on my own from here on.

'Janet, perhaps there is some comment you would like to make before we close our story?'

'Like what? I really wouldn't know where to start.'

'Well, for instance, did you have any idea what Down syndrome was before you had Lee?'

'No, I'd never even heard of it.'

'In that case, how did you feel after having two sons and then giving what seemed like a normal birth to a daughter with Down syndrome?'

'Not a lot really. They explained it all to me, and although I heard what they were saying, I only understood vaguely that she would be slow and that seemed fine. I could cope with that.'

'And when you got home with her?'

'Not much then either. She ate and slept well and there wasn't too much to do. It only started getting busy when at five weeks old she started her swimming lessons.'

'How did your in-laws and grandparents react when they found out about Lee's problem?'

'They were in shock for a while and quite negative really, then slowly they warmed to the idea and, of course, to Lee.'

'After Lee's birth, were you nervous when you became pregnant with Andy?'

'No. I had an amnio test at five months. The doctor gave me no choice about this, even though he told us that having another baby with Down syndrome was unlikely. I suppose he thought it might be too hard for me to manage two children with difficulties.'

'The next few questions may be awkward, even a bit unfair, so don't answer them if you'd rather not, okay? If the test had been positive, do you think you would have carried on with the pregnancy?'

'Don't know the answer to that.'

'When, at what point, did you realise that David had been so deeply affected?'

'Right away. He looked like death when he came in to tell me.'

'How long after you had Lee did you give the future some thought?'

'I really didn't try to think ahead. I don't think like that. You know I'm a today person.'

Janet was not entirely at ease dredging up these memories and I had no wish to make her uncomfortable. She got up to pull the curtain over as the sun was sharp and blinding as it cut into the room.

'Can we carry on or do you want to leave it for now?'

'No, it's fine, I'd rather keep going.'

'Which were some of the most troublesome times you had with Lee?'

'Oh, after she learnt to walk she just kept on getting lost. She'd be standing beside me holding onto my skirt one moment and was nowhere to be seen the next. Taking her shopping was a nightmare. She could wander off at an incredible speed.' Involuntarily Janet shook her head. 'Also the bus station episode was terrible.'

'When did her lack of progress begin to show up?'

'Well the gap began to widen when she couldn't get going to sit up, then stand and then start walking for a much longer time than what seemed to be normal. However, I wasn't surprised because I expected her to be slow.'

'Were your non-Down's parents difficult friends to be with?'

'Never. They were all positive and normal. Lee got invited to their houses to play, and to their children's parties, and their children came to us. It was quite uneventful really.'

'Would you have done anything different with the boys if Lee had not had a problem?'

'I don't think so. All the kids were young enough to do most of the stuff we did together – we all went out in a group or they played in the garden. They swam together, and Lee was the best swimmer of the four of them so they had some respect for that.'

'Were the changes from one country to another, and even from one school to another, traumatic for Lee?'

'No, they were surprisingly easy and uneventful.'

'Now that she's eighteen have you got any particular future planned out for her?'

'Nothing definite really. It's very difficult to be too precise when planning anything for her, although I have been told that she can stay at school until she's twenty-one.'

'And after that?'

'She may go to a technical college for two years, where she can do a specially designed life-skills course.'

'What would that consist of?'

'I haven't gone into the details yet, but I believe it will include things like computing, pottery and gardening — things that go towards filling up a day. It's a Rudolf Steiner type of place. This would occupy about two to three days a week and for the rest of the week she could do some sort of a job.'

'What sort of job?'

'Not sure, but perhaps something like the work she does now at the creche.'

'Will she live there?'

'No, not unless she wants to. I think it would probably be better if she stays at home, but at the same time she needs to spend enough time in the company of a peer group. Of course, things may still change.'

'Janet, how has having Lee affected any plans that you had for your own life?'

Janet laughed. She thought this to be a novel idea.

'I never had any plans. She was lucky.'

'Have the boys ever said anything to you about having a handicapped sister?'

'No… in fact, ever since she was born they've had an incredibly positive reaction.'

'Do you want to say or add anything else?'

'Only that a lot of people seem to think it's all a big deal and it's not – she's not ill or anything. But she is stubborn.'

Then as an afterthought she added, 'And that's her only foible.'

AFTERWORD

WHAT IS DOWN SYNDROME?

A great deal of information describing the various clinical aspects, causes and resultant effects of Down syndrome have been documented and are widely available from papers, books and from a range of Internet sites. It is not my intention to reiterate these facts, but rather to include this piece as a simple reference and explanation of the condition, which may be helpful to readers.

The purpose of telling Lee's story is to promote a wider understanding of its effect on an emerging adult by those of us living ordinary lives and who may at some stage come into contact with someone who has Down syndrome.

What is Down syndrome? Is it preventable or curable? Unfortunately the answer in both cases is "No" — at least, not yet! Down syndrome is not an illness, it is a condition. It is the result of a malfunction of a certain chromosome, which occurs during the early stages of its division. At this time there is no known reversible procedure. Detection of the chromosomal aberration which causes Down syndrome can be made in the early stages of pregnancy by various test procedures. A routine ultrasound carried out at eighteen weeks can also sometimes detect Down syndrome. If detected, the pregnancy can be terminated, but once the child has been born, the condition is irreversible.

The most common type of Down syndrome is caused by an abnormality occurring during the separation process of a particular chromosome, known as chromosome 21. This faulty separation results in the formation of the extra chromosome 21, which becomes present in all the developing cells. This phenomenon is called Trisomy 21. This is a unique event and is not inherited through families.

The genes, which are part of the chromosomal matrix, each represent a specific piece of information. There are usually 46 chromosomes but with Down syndrome there is one extra chromosome in the developing cells, which later become the embryo, the foetus and finally the child who has Down syndrome. Other 'errors' occurring on different chromosomes produce various other types of defects. It is possible that some day a form of genetic engineering may be able to correct these phenomena at source.

A syndrome is not an illness, it is a name given to a combination of signs and symptoms that indicate a particular condition. The child with Down syndrome is therefore not ill, but is limited by the genetic make-up he or she has unwittingly received. Children with Down syndrome are unique human beings with their own personalities, natures, feelings and emotions. A great deal of extra effort and attention is needed to care for and nurture these children. However, like most children, the maturing child with Down syndrome can reward his or her parents with many delightful moments and lasting memories, just as Lee has done for her family.